*"Where rolls the Oregon and hears no sound
Save his own dashings — yet the dead are there!"*

from *"Thanatopsis"* — William Cullen Bryant

Where Rolls The OREGON

Cascade Sundown

**Rick
Steber**

**Bear
Wallow**

**Jerry
Gildemeister**

3

The Bear Wallow Publishing Company
Union, Oregon

A Limited First Printing • 1985

❧ CONTENTS ❧

© 1985 • The Bear Wallow Publishing Company
Copyright and Library of Congress Cataloging-in-Publication Data on page 203.
ISBN 0-936376-03-1

The first European to sight the Pacific Northwest was Sir Francis Drake who cruised along the coast in the 1500s searching for a passage that would return his pirate ship, the *Golden Hind*, eastward to the Atlantic Ocean.

Two hundred years passed before another Englishman, Captain James Cook, visited these shores. On this voyage, quite by accident, his crew discovered sea otter fur was highly prized in China. Trade developed with China and adventurous sea captains from England, Spain, Russia and the United States who traded trinkets to the natives for valuable sea otter fur.

Within a generation the sea otter played out and attention was turned inland. The Columbia River and its tributaries were the trader's earliest highways. The monopolistic Hudson's Bay Company soon gained control and sent trapping expeditions out over the land. These trappers crisscrossed towering forests of thousand-year-old trees, conquered mountain barriers and cut broad sweeps across the high desert in search of beaver and other fur-bearing animals.

They called this big country the "*Columbia District*". It stretched from the Pacific Ocean to the Rocky Mountains, encompassing present-day states of Oregon, Washington, Idaho and portions of Wyoming, Montana, and the province of British Columbia.

Where Rolls The Oregon retraces the footsteps of the early explorers, fur traders, missionaries and settlers. The Oregon country is unveiled as it was found — wild, raw and unrelentingly beautiful.

Mt. Washington

❧ *About the Book* ❧

Researching **Where Rolls The Oregon** involved the study of books, articles, copies of original journals and map reproductions. The manuscript was built around events, happenings, the territorial fight to gain control of the land and the subtle changes that spread across the Pacific Northwest. But more than anything the writing became the story of the people, the extraordinary individuals who challenged themselves and the often unfriendly country.

Rick Steber

Creating **Where Rolls The Oregon** and visually capturing the Oregon country much as I imagined the native Americans, legendary explorers, and trappers would have seen it over 150 years ago has been a tremendous challenge.

Researching old journals and historic maps led to extensive traveling over the Oregon Country for nearly two years searching for historic routes of travel and waiting for those brief moments to capture the moods of the countryside. Then more months were spent in design and mapmaking to merge the visuals with Rick's writing to create a unique blend of story and illustration.

Jerry Gildemeister

Creation of the Oregon Country

Waves rolled the tranquil surface of the shallow Cretaceous sea, breaking the stark reflection of the sun, the clouds and the blue sky.

And then 65 million years ago there was a tremendous upheaval from deep in the earth; the flat continental shelf, under immense pressure, twisted and buckled. Mountains were formed. The sea drained away following two main courses, the Colorado River to the south and the Columbia River to the north. Between these two great systems formed Lake Bonneville, an inland sea.

Columbia River and Mt. Hood

The ocean shoreline traced along the western edge of the emerging Cascade mountain range. Under the ocean floor boiled molten magma seeking weak points in the earth's crust. Cinder cones dotted the interior, a string of volcanoes erupted in the Cascades. Offshore, submarine volcanoes formed the foundation of the coastal mountain range.

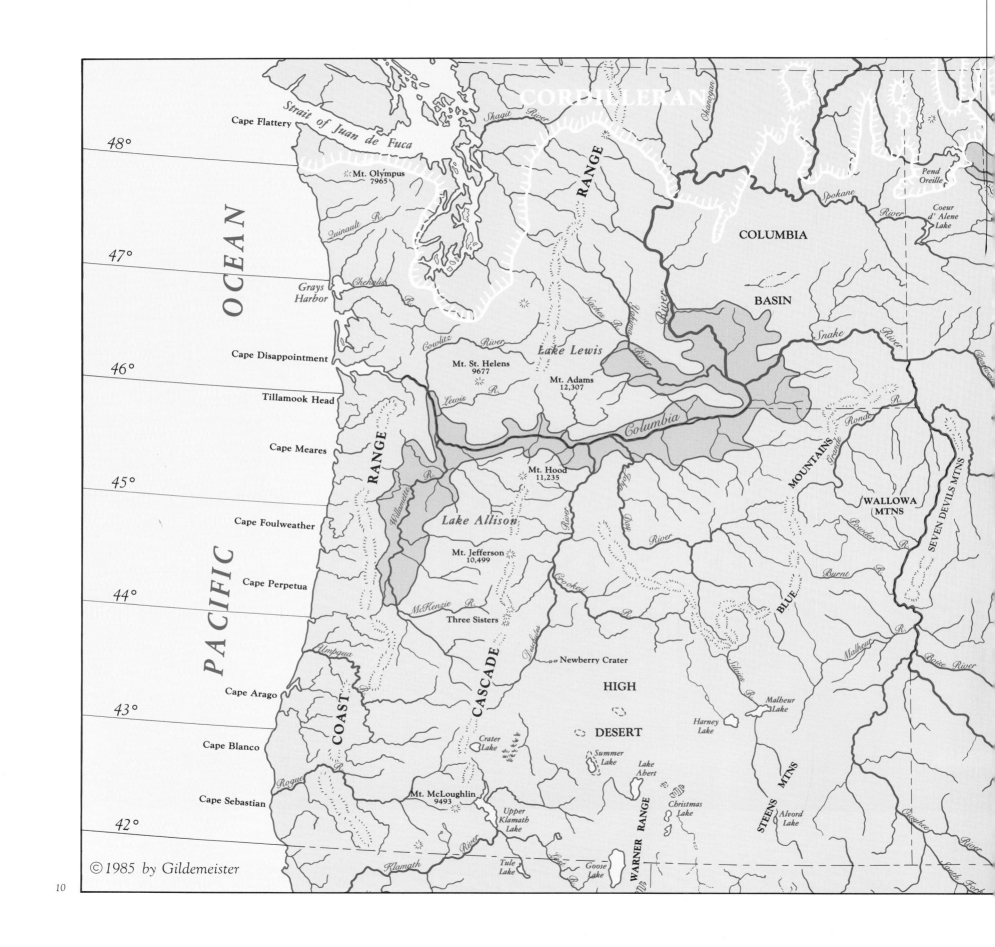

OCEAN

PACIFIC

Cape Flattery

Strait of Juan de Fuca

Mt. Olympus
7965

CORDILLERAN

RANGE

COLUMBIA

BASIN

Skagit River

Okanogan

Pend
Oreille

Spokane

River

Coeur
d' Alene
Lake

Quinault R.

Grays
Harbor

Chehalis

R.

Cape Disappointment

Cowlitz River

Lake Lewis

Mt. St. Helens
9677

Natches R.

Mt. Adams
12,307

Snake River

Tillamook Head

Lewis R.

Cape Meares

RANGE

Columbia

Mt. Hood
11,235

Ronde

MOUNTAINS

Granule

Cape Foulweather

Lake Allison

Willamette R.

River

WALLOWA
MTNS

SEVEN DEVILS MTNS

Cape Perpetua

Mt. Jefferson
10,499

Crooked

River

Burnt R.

BLUE

McKenzie R.

Three Sisters

Deschutes R.

Malheur

Boise River

COAST

Newberry Crater

HIGH

Malheur
Lake

Cape Arago

RANGE

CASCADE

Harney
Lake

Umpqua R.

Cape Blanco

Crater
Lake

DESERT

Summer
Lake

Lake
Abert

Cape Sebastian

Rogue R.

Mt. McLoughlin
9493

Upper
Klamath
Lake

Christmas
Lake

STEENS MTNS

Alvord
Lake

WARNER RANGE

Owyhee River

South Fork

Klamath River

Tule
Lake

Goose
Lake

48°

47°

46°

45°

44°

43°

42°

© 1985 by Gildemeister

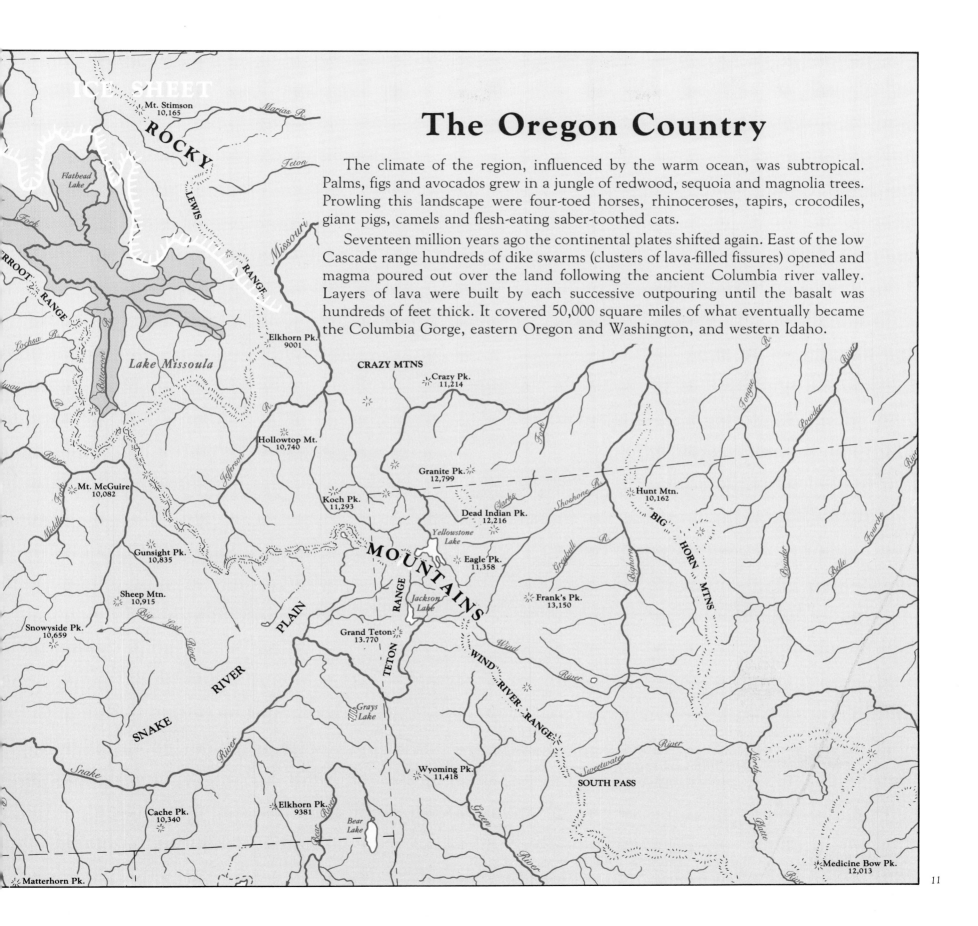

The Oregon Country

The climate of the region, influenced by the warm ocean, was subtropical. Palms, figs and avocados grew in a jungle of redwood, sequoia and magnolia trees. Prowling this landscape were four-toed horses, rhinoceroses, tapirs, crocodiles, giant pigs, camels and flesh-eating saber-toothed cats.

Seventeen million years ago the continental plates shifted again. East of the low Cascade range hundreds of dike swarms (clusters of lava-filled fissures) opened and magma poured out over the land following the ancient Columbia river valley. Layers of lava were built by each successive outpouring until the basalt was hundreds of feet thick. It covered 50,000 square miles of what eventually became the Columbia Gorge, eastern Oregon and Washington, and western Idaho.

ICE SHEET

ROCKY

LEWIS

RANGE

BITTERROOT RANGE

Mt. Stimson
10,165

Flathead Lake

Marias R.

Teton

Missouri

Elkhorn Pk.
9001

Lochsa R.

Lake Missoula

Mt. McGuire
10,082

CRAZY MTNS

Crazy Pk.
11,214

Hollowtop Mt.
10,740

Granite Pk.
12,799

Hunt Mtn.
10,162

BIG

HORN

MTNS

Koch Pk.
11,293

Dead Indian Pk.
12,216

Clarke Fork

Shoshone R.

Tongue R.

Powder River

Yellowstone Lake

Gunsight Pk.
10,835

Eagle Pk.
11,358

Greybull R.

Sheep Mtn.
10,915

Frank's Pk.
13,150

Bighorn River

Belle Fourche

MOUNTAINS

Jackson Lake

Snowyside Pk.
10,659

Big Lost River

RIVER

PLAIN

TETON RANGE

Grand Teton
13,770

WIND

RIVER

RANGE

Wind River

SNAKE

Grays Lake

Snake River

Wyoming Pk.
11,418

Sweetwater River

SOUTH PASS

Cache Pk.
10,340

Elkhorn Pk.
9381

Bear Lake

Green River

Sandy

Platte River

Matterhorn Pk.

Medicine Bow Pk.
12,013

The Columbia River Basalt is divided into five distinct lava flows. The oldest, Imnaha, was restricted to western Idaho and northeastern Oregon. The next oldest was Picture Gorge, confined to the John Day country of Oregon. The other three, Grande Ronde, Wanapum and Saddle Mountain, are known collectively as the Yakima Basalt. They flowed one on top of another. Covering by far the largest area was the Grande Ronde which originated from dike swarms in the mountainous region of northeast Oregon and flowed westward, filling the low areas as it slowly coursed down the broad Columbia valley to eventually reach the sea in the vicinity of Astoria. Later outpourings, Wanapum and Saddle Mountain, covered smaller areas but like the Grande Ronde they forced the Columbia River to change course and flow farther to the north.

After the last major flow there was perhaps a million years of relative calm. Then dozens of Cascade volcanoes erupted at once. Shields of gray basalt oozed from craters and narrowed the gorge through which the Columbia River passed. Within this time frame there was a gigantic upheaval and the Coast and Cascade ranges up-arched and other areas down-folded to make basins and valleys.

12

Painted Hills

The rise of the mountain arches signaled a dramatic change in weather patterns. Storms dropped their moisture on the west side of the Cascades. To the east extended a rain shadow, the climate became semi-arid and much cooler causing extinction of many forms of plant and animal life. Eventually the basalt eroded, grassy plains developed and were roamed by elephants, horses, rhinoceroses, camels, antelopes, bears, mammoths and mastodons.

Two million years ago there was another climatic change, possibly brought on by swirling clouds of volcanic ash. The earth began to cool. An Ice Age dawned and covered half the North American continent under a glacier. Consequently, the sea level dropped at least 300 feet.

The Cordilleran Ice Sheet advanced into northern portions of the Columbia river drainage and retreated, advanced and retreated, each time temporarily damming the river. The largest of these dams, and the last, occurred about 13,000 years ago. Behind a wall of ice one thousand feet thick a 3,000 square mile lake, Lake Missoula, was formed. When the climate began to warm, the height of the dam was reduced and water flowed over the top. In a matter of hours it cut through the ice dam and unleashed the most catastrophic flood of all time.

Glaciated Wallowa Mountains

In the Big Bend country of eastern Washington the flood cascaded over a sheer basalt cliff at a rate in excess of nine cubic miles of water per hour for at least 40 hours. When the water receded it left behind a multitude of barren channels and dry falls.

At the Wallula Gap the flood crested at a height of 1,200 feet and spread out into twin lakes, Lake Lewis on the north and Lake Condon on the south, before squeezing through the Columbia Gorge. The emerging water charged up the Willamette Valley, forming 400-foot deep Lake Allison, before bleeding down the Columbia channel to the sea.

Obsidian Flow

The sea, thick with the milky-brown glacial runoff, was on the rise. It drowned the 25-mile wide coastal plain. Waves tore at the foothills of the coastal range, eroding the loose soil and leaving jagged monoliths, lonely sentinels facing the brilliant setting sun.

Monolith Sunset

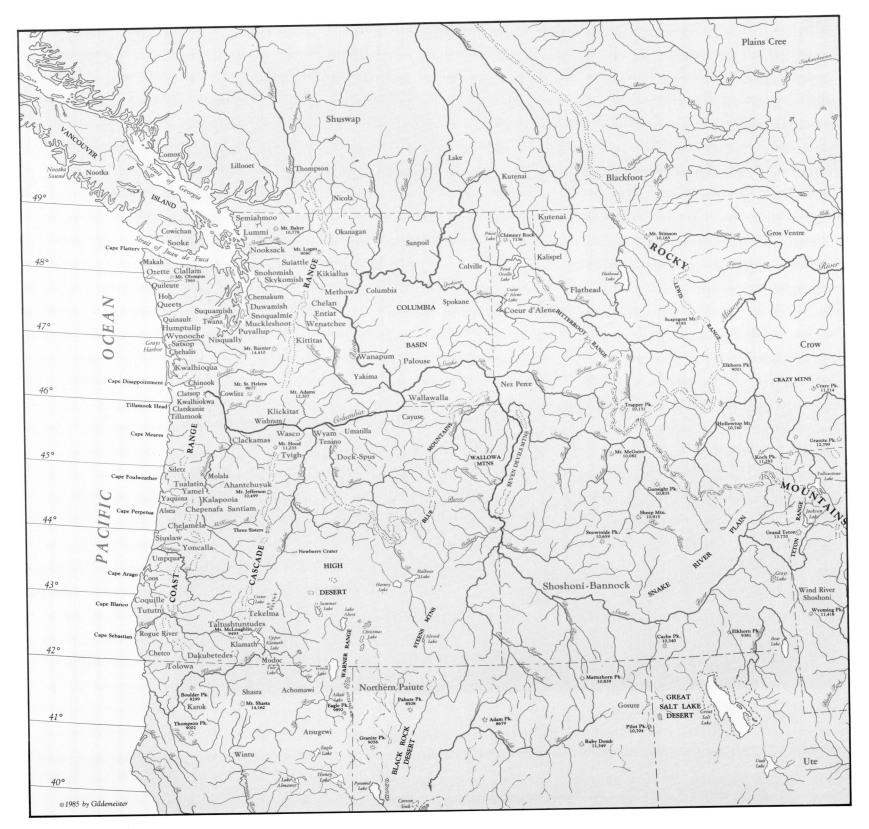

Plains Cree

VANCOUVER ISLAND

Shuswap

Comox

Nootka
Sound Nootka

Lillooet

Thompson

Lake

Kutenai

Blackfoot

49°

Semiahmoo
Lummi Mt. Baker
10,778

Nicola

Okanagan

Kutenai

Mt. Stimson
10,165

Gros Ventre

ROCKY

Cowichan
Sooke

Nooksack

Sanpoil

Strait of Juan de Fuca

48°

Cape Flattery
Makah

Mt. Logan
9080

Suiattle

Colville

Kalispel

Chimney Rock
7136

Priest
Lake

Ozette Clallam
Mt. Olympus
7965

Snohomish Kikiallus
Skykomish

Methow Columbia

Spokane

Coeur d'Alene
d'Alene
Lake

Flathead

Flathead
Lake

Quileute
Hoh
Queets

Chemakum
Duwamish
Suquamish Snoqualmie
Twana Muckleshoot
Puyallup

Chelan
Entiat
Wenatchee

COLUMBIA

Coeur d'Alene

BITTERROOT

Scapegoat Mt.
9185

47°

Quinault
Humptulip
Wynooche
Grays Satsop
Harbor Chehalis

Nisqually

Kittitas

BASIN

Palouse

Snake

Elkhorn Pk.
9001

Crow

CRAZY MTNS

46°

Kwalhioqua

Chinook
Clatsop
Cape Disappointment Kwalhiokwa
Tillamook Head Clatskanie
Tillamook

Mt. Rainier
14,410

Mt. St. Helens
9677

Cowlitz

Mt. Adams
12,307

Wanapum

Yakima

Wallawalla

Nez Perce

Trapper Pk.
10,131

Crazy Pk.
11,214

Cayuse

Columbia

Hollowtop Mt
10,740

45°

Cape Meares

Wishram

Wasco Wyam
Clackamas Tenino

Umatilla

WALLOWA
MTNS

Mt. McGuire
10,082

Granite Pk.
12,799

Cape Foulweather

Siletz

Molala

Mt. Hood
11,235

Tyigh

Dock-Spus

MOUNTAINS

Koch Pk.
11,293

44°

Cape Perpetua

Tualatin
Yamel
Yaquina Kalapooia
Alsea Chepenafa Santiam
Chelamela

Ahantchuyuk
Mt. Jefferson
10,499

BLUE

SEVEN DEVILS MTNS

Gunsight Pk.
10,835

Yellowstone
Lake

MOUNTAINS

43°

Siuslaw
Yoncalla

Three Sisters

Sheep Mtn.
10,915

Grand Teton
13,770

Jackson
Lake

TETON RANGE

Umpqua
Cape Arago Coos
Coquille
Tututni

Newberry Crater

HIGH

Snowyside Pk.
10,659

RIVER

PLAIN

Cape Blanco

Tekelma

DESERT

Malheur
Lake

Shoshoni-Bannock

SNAKE

Grays
Lake

42°

Cape Sebastian

Taltushtuntudes
Mt. McLoughlin
9493

Rogue River

Chetco Dakubetedes

Tolowa

Crater
Lake

Summer
Lake

Harney
Lake

Lake
Abert

Klamath
Modoc

Upper
Klamath
Lake

STEENS MTNS

Alvord
Lake

Cache Pk.
10,340

Elkhorn Pk.
9381

Bear
Lake

Wind River
Shoshoni

Wyoming Pk.
11,418

Tule
Lake

Goose
Lake

WARNER RANGE

Christmas
Lake

Matterhorn Pk.
10,839

41°

Boulder Pk.
8299
Karok

Shasta

Achomawi

Mt. Shasta
14,162

Eagle Pk.
9892

Alkali
Lake

Northern Paiute

Pahute Pk.
8508

Adam Pk.
8679

Gosute

GREAT
SALT LAKE
DESERT

Pilot Pk.
10,704

Great
Salt
Lake

Thompson Pk.
9002

Atsugewi

Granite Pk.
9056

BLACK ROCK DESERT

Ruby Dome
11,349

Ute

Utah
Lake

40°

Wintu

Lake
Almanor

Honey
Lake

Pyramid
Lake

Carson
Sink

OCEAN

PACIFIC

COAST RANGE

CASCADE RANGE

© 1985 by Gildemeister

16

The First Inhabitants

According to popular theory Asians migrated over an ice bridge between continents to arrive in North America between 35,000 to 100,000 years ago. These natives endured the later stages of the Ice Age, withstood the catastrophic flood of the Columbia River and witnessed volcanic eruptions and red-hot lava bubbling from the ground.

The Chinook Indian version of their own creation, a story passed through generations, was that an old woman and two young girls walked to the lower Columbia River from a land far to the north. One day the girls were sitting on a large stone wishing for husbands so they might have children, when a man appeared. He told them if they looked into the other world they would see their husbands. He made the earth open and the girls looked down and saw the apparition of two men surrounded by fire. They were frightened and ran away. They told the old woman what they had seen and she, too, was alarmed. That night while the girls slept they were visited by the men of fire who disappeared into the morning sky and became stars. The girls followed, but sent their children from the sky and they became the Chinooks.

Chinook Lodge

It has been estimated that 100,000 Indians were living in the Oregon country at the coming of the first white man. They were arranged by tribe, speaking one of sixteen distinct languages. In the interior the tribes were accustomed to moving with the changing food supply depending on the season, while the coastal tribes existed in permanent camps.

The great gorge of the Columbia River opened a natural gateway between the seacoast and the interior. A system of barter was developed through the land from the Pacific to the Rocky Mountains. The river also enabled the salmon to reach spawning grounds far upstream. The salmon provided an abundant supply of food and when runs were on Indians gathered at the falls of the Columbia Gorge to dip net or spear salmon as they leaped from the water in their struggle upstream. Many tribes were represented and temporary camps swelled to populations of several thousand. The Indians fished, gambled, raced horses and bartered for items common to particular regions: camas root, wapato root, native tobacco, bear grass for basket making and flint for arrowheads.

Camas

Chinook legend holds that Talipus, a god, broke down the mountains which had prevented salmon from ascending the rivers and created rapids and cascades which compelled the fish to leap so they could be taken by the Indians. He also directed where the different tribes should live and instructed them in the modes of catching fish — seine in the lower river, the dip net in the rapids above.

A way of life that existed for countless centuries was destroyed by the coming of the white man and his diseases. The native population had no immunity and was swept away. Along the lower Columbia River, among the Chinook tribes, the death rate reached 95%. Entire villages were exterminated.

Nathaniel Wyeth, an American trapper and trader, made note in his journal April 3, 1835, on the desolation of Sauvie Island at the confluence of the Willamette and Columbia rivers: "*A mortality has carried off to a man its inhabitants, and there is nothing to attest that they ever existed, except their decaying houses, their graves and their unburied bones, of which there are heaps.*"

Salmon Jumping

19

Sketch'd by J. Drayton   Jordan & Halpin sc.

WILLAMETTE FALLS

That same year another traveler, John K. Townsend, wrote: *"The depopulation has been truly fearful. A gentleman told me that only four years ago [1831], as he wandered near what had been formerly a thickly peopled village, he counted no less than sixteen dead men and women, lying unburied and festering in the sun in front of their habitations. Within the houses, all were sick; not one had escaped the contagion; upwards of a hundred individuals, men, women and children, were writhing in agony on the floors of their houses, with no one to render them any assistance. Some were in the dying struggle, and clenching with the convulsive gasp of death their disease-worn companions, shrieked and howled in the last sharp agony.*

"Probably there does not now exist one, where five years ago there were a hundred Indians; and in sailing up the river, from the cape to the Cascades, the only evidence of the existence of the Indian is an occasional miserable wigwam, with a few wretched half-starved occupants."

Plagues unleashed by the white intruders included smallpox, fever and ague, tuberculosis, measles and venereal diseases. By 1846, the year the United States and Great Britain agreed upon the Oregon boundary, the native population had been reduced to fewer than 15,000. These survivors, so few in number and spread over a large territory, gave little resistance as the pioneers came in and took control of the land.

Sir George Simpson, western governor of Hudson's Bay Company, wrote in 1841 of visiting the Columbia River: *"The shores were silent and solitary, the deserted villages forming melancholy monuments of the generation that had passed away."*

Discovery of a New World

Buried among documents of China's Sung Dynasty is an astounding tale of discovery. According to the report a Buddhist priest, Hwui Shan, and four other priests sailed from mainland China in 458 A.D. on a voyage to carry the light of Buddhism to the unknown corners of the world.

Favorable winds and a strong ocean current carried the priests' small craft on a north and easterly course. Forty years passed before Hwui Shan returned to China, the only survivor of the journey. He told fantastic stories about islands he named *Country of Marked Bodies*, which could have been the Aleutian chain, and a continent he called *Fu-sang*, possibly the coast of North America. Hwui Shan convinced the Chinese emperor his story was true and his words were added to the official records of the dynasty.

A translation of Hwui Shan's story includes his observations that: "*The ground* [in Fu-sang] *is destitute of iron, but they have copper. Gold and silver are not valued. In their markets there are no taxes or fixed prices....The people have no weapons, and do not make war. According to the laws of the kingdom, there is a southern prison and a northern prison. Those who have committed crimes that are not very serious are sent to the southern prison, but great criminals are placed in the northern prison, and are afterward transferred into that of the south, if they obtain their pardon; otherwise they are condemned to remain all their lives in the first. They are permitted to marry, but their children are made slaves....*

"*In matters of marriage it is the law the man wishing to marry must clear the ground before the hut of the woman he desires for a year and if the woman is not pleased with him she sends him away; but if they are mutually pleased the marriage is complete.*"

Hwui Shan said he traveled among the people of Fu-sang and spread the teachings of Buddha: "*The laws, canons, and images of my faith were made known. Priests of regular ordination were set apart among the natives, and the customs of the country became reformed.*"

The detailed account of Hwui Shan has led many historians to conclude that he was the true discoverer of the North American continent. From a study of ocean currents and the geography of the coastline it is obvious such a voyage was possible. A warm ocean current follows a route from the coast of China, past the northern islands of Japan to the Aleutian chain and south along the coast of North America. Nowhere are points of land more than 200 miles apart.

Proof that a ship set adrift in the Japanese current would reach the eastern shore of the Pacific was established when a junk, carrying a crew of 14 men and a cargo of rice and porcelainware, was driven off course between Japanese islands by a typhoon. The storm damaged her rudder so she could not be steered. At the mercy of the current and Pacific storms, the junk was driven northeasterly. The crew, though they had plenty of rice and water, suffered from beriberi and all but three perished at sea.

For a year they drifted before the junk came in sight of land off Cape Flattery in January 1834. The junk was broken up by a storm but the three survivors were washed ashore, captured and made slaves by the natives.

News of the wreck passed among tribes until Dr. John McLoughlin, Chief Factor of the Hudson's Bay post at Fort Vancouver, was notified. He immediately dispatched a party of 30 men to search for wreckage and any evidence of survivors. Because of bad weather and the rugged coastline the party turned back before reaching Cape Flattery.

Dr. McLoughlin then dispatched the company ship *Lama* to investigate. The three Japanese were located and brought to Fort Vancouver. The captain of the *Lama* reported the Indians *"were much inclined to keep these men in slavery"* but that they were able to persuade the Indians to release the Japanese after *"suitable reward"* was made as an *"inducement to treat with kindness others in like condition in the future."*

In November when the *Eagle* sailed for London with the annual cargo of furs, she carried on deck the survivors who finally returned to their homeland in 1837.

The saga of the Japanese junk illustrates that a ship, at the mercy of the ocean current and storms, could eventually reach the North Pacific coast. It helps substantiate Hwui Shan's claim as the original discoverer of the North American continent.

Legend of the Stone Face

According to Clatsop Indian legend, at some prehistoric time there was a shipwreck at the mouth of the Columbia River. Two men made it to shore—strange men with white skin, flaming red hair and bushy beards.

The storm passed and seagulls wheeled over the crashing breakers picking up anything edible from the wreckage. The two men stood beside a roaring driftwood fire and the curious Indians pressed close. The white men spotted them and with encouraging signs invited the natives to the campfire. The strangers popped corn and showed the Indians by example they should eat it. The popped corn was new and delicious and the Indians assumed these visitors were sent by the Great Spirit that lived beyond the ocean where the sun slept.

The men were given names, Kunupi and Soto. They took wives and for several years resided in the village. They taught the Indians how to shape metal for ornaments, tools and weapons. But Kunupi and Soto were never completely happy. They spoke of their own race and made sign they lived far to the east. At last, early one spring, they turned their backs on the village of the Clatsops and began a journey upriver to the east. They were never seen by the Clatsops again.

At the turn of this century an artifact was discovered along the lower Columbia River, a stone sculpted in the likeness of a Caucasian man with a full beard. The solemn face, marred by patches of lichen — could it be the stone head of Kunupi or Soto?

23

Sir Francis Drake—1578
In the Ship *Golden Hind.*

Capt. James Cook—1778
In the Ships *Resolution & Discovery.*

Capt. George Vancouver—1792
In the Ships *Discovery & Chatham.*

Sea Exploration

The first European to behold the Pacific Ocean was Vasco Nunez de Balboa in 1513. From a hilltop at the Isthmus of Panama he named this vast body of water *Mar del Sur* (Sea of the South) and laid claim to all the land the waters broke upon in the name of Spain.

Seven years later Ferdinand Magellan, also under the Spanish flag, discovered a southern passage around the tip of South America. He entered a great, calm sea and named it the Pacific Ocean.

The conquistadors arrived in South and Central America to rob it of its riches and the Pacific was claimed as a limitless Spanish lake into which all other nations were forbidden to sail.

The Spaniards went in search of a northwest passage. Juan Rodriguez Cabrillo was sent on an expedition to locate this passage in 1542. He reached a latitude of 38 degrees north before suddenly becoming ill and dying. His pilot, Bartolome Ferrelo, assumed command and the expedition continued to near the 42nd parallel before being driven south by storms.

Pacific Sunrise

In the succeeding six decades, during which the Spanish Armada was destroyed, there was no publicized exploration of the North Pacific coast. However, in later years a Greek sailor named Apostolos Valerianus, but commonly called Juan de Fuca, came forward with an account that he had been employed by the Viceroy of Mexico to explore for a northwest passage. Although his story was never substantiated, Juan de Fuca related that as captain of a small caravel he had discovered, between latitudes 47 and 48 degrees, a broad inland sea (Strait of Juan de Fuca) upon which he sailed for twenty days without locating the outlet.

Sir Francis Drake

Sir Francis Drake was the most daring and dashing of all pirates, the Terror of the Spanish Main.

In 1577 Drake departed England in command of a pirate force of five ships and 164 men ostensibly bound for Alexandria. Once out of sight of land, Drake altered the course and told his crew the object of the voyage was the faraway Pacific, the private sea of King Philip of Spain and his galleons of South American gold.

Only three ships successfully navigated the treacherous Strait of Magellan — the *Marygold*, the *Elizabeth* and Drake's ship, the *Pelican*, which he rechristened the *Golden Hind* upon entering the Pacific.

The fleet started north up the coast but a fierce tempest struck and, adding more terror to the night, the moon eclipsed. For two weeks the storm raged before blowing itself out. When the seas calmed the *Golden Hind* was alone on the broad Pacific. With a fresh wind filling her sails she started north, a Spanish flag flying from her mast.

The first ship they encountered was a treasure ship about to set sail for Panama where the cargo would be transferred overland to the Atlantic. Sailors on board assumed the vessel flying the Spanish flag was one of their own, never considering it could be the monster Drake last seen six years earlier on the Spanish Main.

The *Golden Hind* drew alongside and Drake and his crew were welcomed aboard to share a drink of wine. The Englishmen graciously accepted but at once made their identity known and taunted the outmanned Spaniards with, *"Go down you dogs! Swim for it!"* One man jumped in the water and the remainder were set on shore as the prize ship was stripped of gold and 1,770 jars of wine.

The *Golden Hind* overtook a richly-laden ship, *Our Lady of the Conception*, north of the harbor of Callao de Lima. From her the pirates transferred to their ship 13 chests of coined silver, 26 tons of silver bars, 80 pounds of gold, and treasure chests overflowing with pearls.

Rather than running the gauntlet returning to England the way he had come, Drake continued north hoping to discover a passage to the Atlantic. But the land Drake named *Nova Albion* (New England) extended without interruption.

By summer of 1579 the pirate ship was off the coast of Oregon. Farther north the *Golden Hind* ran into cold weather — so cold the rigging was covered with ice and the crew, fresh from the Tropics, pleaded with the captain to turn back. But Drake was determined to find a passage. Accounts of the voyage reported that a latitude of 48 degrees north (to Vancouver Island) was reached before Drake gave the order to turn back.

Under the tons of plunder the *Golden Hind* was leaking badly at the seams and finally had to put in at a harbor along the coast for repairs. Here Drake went ashore and claimed this land in the name of Queen Elizabeth.

After spending 37 days with repairs in Nova Albion, Drake put to sea and pointed his ship southwest to the trade winds. Fourteen months later, after a voyage of nearly three years, the *Golden Hind* sailed into Plymouth Sound, her keel completing a furrow that encompassed the world.

Spanish Exploration

King Philip III was crowned King of Spain in 1598. One of his first acts was to order an expedition be sent to the Pacific Northwest coast in search of the secret Northwest Passage.

Sebastian Viscaino, chief pilot in His Majesty's service, was chosen to head the expedition which departed Acapulco and sailed north bucking gusty winds and rough, rolling seas. Viscaino reported in his log that at one time only two sailors of his entire crew were capable of climbing to the main top sail. The others were confined to their bunks, too sick and feeble to risk being on deck.

Viscaino turned his ship, the *Capitana*, south with the hope of outrunning the raging series of storms that marched in one after another. The other ship, the *fragata* in command of Martin de Aguilar, held her position. When the wind finally shifted, it came straight from the south blowing a gale. The *fragata* ran with it. The storm subsided and Aguilar swung east. On January 19, 1603, he spotted a point of land in the latitude of 43 degrees and named it Cape Blanco.

Aguilar claimed in this vicinity he also discovered a broad and abundant flowing river. He speculated he had located the fabled *Strait of Anian* (the Northwest Passage) and attempted to run the *fragata* over the bar. The current proved too strong and the ship was ordered to stand off coast and await more favorable conditions. Before another effort could be made, a violent storm blew out of the north and drove the *fragata* south.

During the next 170 years there were no Spanish expeditions sent to verify Aguilar's claim. At this time Spain was in a state of gradual decline and was disposed to protect her interests in Mexico and California. Rather than expanding her territories, Spain fought to hold on to what she had and entered an era of intense colonization, building a string of missions and, in effect, proving her authority to Mexico and California.

In the late 1700s when other countries — Russia, England and France — began showing interest in the North Pacific, Spain again mounted a challenge. Juan Perez headed an expedition that sailed up the coast and reached a higher latitude than had any other Spaniard, the 54th parallel. They put in to a comfortable harbor and were immediately surrounded by natives paddling canoes, very eager to trade sea otter fur. Perez had few trade goods aboard, was skeptical of the value of sea otter fur, and refused to trade.

A second expedition was dispatched and included the ship *Santiago* under command of Bruno Heceta and the schooner *Sonora* under Juan Francisco de la Bodega y Quadra. They set a course far out to sea, veering east after striking the 47th parallel. They approached land and dispatched a boat to obtain a supply of fresh water and berries if possible. The men were suffering with scurvy, a disease caused by a deficiency of vitamin C and characterized by bleeding gums, bleeding under the skin and extreme fatigue.

No sooner did the keel touch soft sand than natives swooped down and killed every man. The savages took up canoes and launched an attack on the *Sonora* but the *Santiago* came to her aid and drove the natives away.

Because of the attack and sickness, the *Sonora's* able-bodied crew was reduced to five seamen and a cabin boy, but they did manage to hoist sail. Heceta was anxious to return to Mexico, but Quadra favored continuing still farther north.

A storm rose and separated the vessels. Heceta seized the opportunity and slipped away, sailing south. On August 17, 1775, (near the 46th parallel) Heceta noted in his journal: *"On the evening of this day I discovered a large bay, to which I gave the name Assumption Bay....*

"Having arrived opposite this bay at six in the evening and placed the ship nearly midway between the two capes, I sounded and found bottom in four brazas [nearly four fathoms]. The currents and eddies were so strong that, notwithstanding a press of sail, it was difficult to get clear of the northern cape, toward which the current ran, though its direction was eastward in consequence of the tide being at flood. These currents and eddies caused me to believe that the place is the mouth of some great river, or of some passage to another sea...."

This was the first recognizable description written about the mouth of the *Great River of the West* but Heceta, in his impatience to return to Mexico, failed to explore the source and therefore missed receiving credit for discovering the Columbia River.

Quadra, in his small vessel of 27 feet with his decimated crew, reached the 50th parallel before abandoning the expedition. The *Sonora* arrived at San Blas, Mexico, November 20, 1775, after an eight-month absence.

The days of Spanish exploration, for the most part, were over. It had been 260 years since Balboa first glimpsed the Pacific Ocean from the hilltop in Panama. During that time, fifteen Spanish government-sponsored expeditions were sent to explore the North Pacific coast. They had been nothing more than superficial explorations; only the most prominent landmarks had been named.

Captain James Cook

British Parliament, in 1776, offered a reward of 20,000 pounds sterling to any captain of a privately owned or Royal Navy ship that could prove the existence of the Northwest Passage.

In an attempt to win the reward as well as to secure the Northwest Passage — if it did exist — for England, two of His Majesty's ships, the *Resolution* and the *Discovery*, were fitted for the long voyage to the Pacific. The ships, under the command of Captain James Cook, sailed from Plymouth Harbor, England, on July 12, 1776.

During the voyage the Sandwich Islands (Hawaiian Islands) were discovered and named in honor of the first lord of the admiralty, the Earl of Sandwich. Following an easterly and northeasterly course from the islands, the watch spotted two whales on March 6, 1778. The following day, at the latitude of 44 degrees, 33 minutes, north, land was sighted at a distance of seventy or eighty miles.

That afternoon a terrific storm rose and made it necessary for the ships to run southward with it. At the height of this storm, with the wind whipping the tops of the tall waves, they were swept close to land. Through the mist there appeared a rugged shoreline and a jagged, rocky point Captain Cook named Cape Foulweather.

Cape Foulweather

They were driven below the 43rd parallel before the storm abated and allowed them to turn north. For three weeks they ranged along the coast, alternately caught in the blustery March storms or beset by calms between storms, searching for a break in the rocky shoreline that would signal the mouth of a passage between the Pacific and Atlantic oceans. But the coast appeared without an inlet or opening. The hills were covered by a dark green forest and the straight north-south coastline was broken only by an occasional promontory or cape.

Captain Cook missed the mouth of the Columbia River. He continued north and on March 22, 1778, wrote that a small round hill ahead gave the appearance of an island and *"there appeared to be a small opening which flattered us with hopes of finding a harbor. On this account I called the point of land to the north of it Cape Flattery."*

Near the 50th parallel a fine harbor offering protection from the weather was observed and the *Resolution* and *Discovery* slipped into it. The sails were hauled in, the anchors dropped. Immediately, a large number of decoratively carved dugout canoes pushed off from the tree-lined shore making straight for the ships. Thirty-two canoes were counted with three to seven wild-looking natives in each. They wore brass rings through their noses, tightly woven baskets on their heads and animal skins covering their bodies.

They encircled the ships. One by one the leaders stood in the canoes and made lengthy speeches in their native tongue. The presentation was concluded with a song. According to the Englishmen the singing carried a very agreeable air with a nice melody. Captain Cook made friendly gestures but the natives were content to sit in their canoes, which they did the greater part of the night.

The following day a cove was selected and the ships anchored there. Hawsers were fastened to trees on shore while the crews made necessary repairs. Here great numbers of natives in a hundred canoes, some manned by as many as 17 Indians, crowded around the ships in the small cove. A few of the more courageous natives were induced to come on board. They mixed with the crew and watched them go about their repair duty with much interest.

Soon the natives were showing items they wished to barter: skins of bears, wolves, foxes and particularly, sea otters. The narrative of the voyage states: *"Besides the skins in their native state, they also brought garments made of them, and another sort of clothing made of the bark of a tree or some plant like hemp; weapons, such as bows, arrows and spears, pieces of carved work, beads and several other little ornaments of thin brass and iron, shaped like a horseshoe, which they hang at their noses. But the most extraordinary of all the articles which they brought to the ship for sale were human skulls and hands, not yet quite stripped of flesh, which they made our people plainly understand they had eaten; and, indeed, some of them had evident marks that they had been upon the fire."*

The natives were described as *"so encrusted with paint and dirt that their color could not positively be determined...they rub their bodies over constantly with a red paint of a course ochrey or clayey substance, their garments contract a rancid, offensive smell and a greasy nastiness, so that they make a very wretched dirty appearance."*

Captain Cook named the harbor Friendly Cove but the natives informed him their name for it was *Nootka*. Repairs were completed and on the 26th of April the ships were ready to depart. The moorings were cast off and the natives departed, climbing down to canoes brought alongside. The last to leave was a chief who had become quite friendly with Captain Cook. In return for a small present he bestowed on Cook a beaver skin of much greater value. Captain Cook made another small present to the chief. In turn the chief removed the fur cloak he was wearing and presented it to the captain.

Captain Cook wrote: *"Struck with this generosity...I presented to him a new broadsword, with a brass hilt, the possession of which made him completely happy. He also, and many of his countrymen, importuned us to pay them another visit, and by way of encouragement promised to lay in a good stock of skins. I make no doubt that whoever comes to this place will find the natives prepared with no inconsiderable supply of an article of trade which they could observe we were eager to possess, and which we found could be purchased to great advantage."*

No sooner did the ships depart Nootka than a storm struck and they bore away from land and out to sea. Not until nearing the 60th parallel did they again sight land. A landing party was sent to shore and here, at the foot of a tree, Captain Cook left a bottle with a paper inside inscribed with the date of discovery and two silver twopence dated 1772.

The expedition continued searching for the Northwest Passage to a latitude of 70 degrees, 44 minutes, where a wall of ice, as far as the eye could see, blocked their path. Here were walruses and Captain Cook wrote: *"They lay in herds of many hundreds upon the ice, huddling one over the other like swine, and roar or bray very loud, so that in the night of foggy weather they gave us notice of the vicinity of ice before we could see it....that as the season was now so far advanced and frost expected soon to set in, it was not considered consistent with prudence to make further attempts to find a passage to the Atlantic."*

The Cook expedition turned its back on the Arctic and sailed for the Sandwich Islands where they intended to winter. There, in Kealakekua Bay on February 14, 1779, Captain Cook attempted to recover a ship's boat stolen by natives. He was attacked and clubbed to death before any of his crew could come to his rescue.

Captain Clerke of the *Discovery* assumed command. They sailed from the islands and, with summer advancing, returned to the Arctic. The wall of ice was as absolutely impenetrable as the year before. Captain Clerke died upon the Siberian coast August 22, 1779, and command fell to Captain Gore. The ships proceeded to Canton, China, and they discovered the furs they had collected along the North Pacific coast were in great demand among the Chinese. Fabulous prices were paid. The crew wanted to procure more furs immediately, but Captain Gore ordered the return to England.

They arrived the following year and reported the riches awaiting individuals brave enough to initiate trade between the North Pacific coast and China. The government suppressed the information at first but rumors spread and the era of the sea trader dawned.

31

Pacific Sundown

The Sea Otter

"For the purpose of hunting the sea otter two very small canoes are prepared, in each of which are two expert hunters. The instruments they [the natives] employ on this occasion are bows and arrows and a small harpoon.... Thus equipped, the hunters proceed among the rocks in search of their prey. Sometimes they surprise him sleeping on his back, on the surface of the water; and, if they can get near the animal without awakening him, which requires infinite precaution, he is easily harpooned and dragged to the boat, when a fierce battle very often ensues between the otter and the hunter, who are frequently wounded by the claws and teeth of the animal."

Captain John Meares
Sea Trader

Russian & English Traders

With the rise to power of Peter the Great, Russia began to look for ways to expand her borders. In 1724, Peter the Great commissioned Vitus Bering, a Danish naval officer, to explore the Siberian coast and the waters of the North Pacific.

Bering and his men traveled by dog team, suffering from the cold and hardship of dragging cables, rigging and anchors across 2,000 miles to the coast of Siberia. There the dogs pulled logs from the forest and lumber was hand-hewn and fitted together to build the *Gabriel*. The *Gabriel* was launched July 13, 1728. A voyage was made that year and one the following year, after which Bering wrote that he had *"ascertained that there really does exist a northwest passage...."*

In 1741 Bering set sail on an ill-fated voyage of discovery in the *St. Peter*. He explored the northern regions and came down the coast of North America to a latitude of 59 degrees, 40 minutes. Here, his crew disabled by scurvy, he turned around. The *St. Peter* wrecked on an island in the Aleutian chain; Bering died but some of his crew survived. When they escaped the island, they took with them a few of the beautiful sea otter pelts they had acquired from the natives.

The furs created a great deal of interest in Siberia and the Russians initiated a number of trading voyages through the middle and late 1700s. These daring Russian seamen braved the fog-bound, treacherous waters of the North Pacific. It has been estimated one out of three wrecked on the rocky coast or struck an island. For the most part the Russians stayed far to the north of the Oregon country and went about collecting furs quietly.

The British divided the world between two giant sea-trade monopolies, the East India Company and the South Sea Company. Rival companies or independent traders sailing under the British flag could not legally trade in China or on the North Pacific coast. British sea captains, tempted by the promise of wealth in the fur trade, began to sail under the flag of competing nations.

The first was James Hanna. His ship was outfitted in China by English merchants and sailed under Portuguese papers. The *Harmon*, a small brig, departed China in April 1785 and arrived at Nootka by August. It returned to China with over $20,000 worth of sea otter fur.

The next traders arrived at Nootka in British vessels, the *Captain Cook* and the *Experiment*, in 1786 under a license granted by the East India Company. Before sailing with a cargo of furs it was decided to leave an agent on the coast. Dr. John Mackay, the surgeon on the *Captain Cook*, volunteered and was let off with instructions to begin stockpiling furs. He lived with the natives and took a native wife.

The next year Captain Charles William Barkley, an Englishman operating under the Austrian flag, arrived on the Northwest coast in command of *The Imperial Eagle*. His wife accompanied him on the voyage, the first white woman to visit these shores.

Mrs. Barkley stood on deck when they dropped anchor in Nootka Sound. A canoe came alongside and she was astonished when one of the natives, a dark-skinned man, dirty and dressed in a sea otter robe, called to her in perfect English. He introduced himself as Dr. John Mackay and asked permission to come on board. Mackay, the first European known to reside among the natives, was offered the opportunity by Captain Barkley to return to civilization. He declined, remarking that the native diet of dried fish and whale oil suited him.

In 1786 Captain John Meares, a retired lieutenant of the British navy, departed Bengal with two ships under his command, the *Nootka* and the *Sea-otter*. The ships did not cross together but arranged to rendezvous in Prince William Sound. Upon his arrival Meares found the *Sea-otter* had been there and departed. Her crew was never heard from again.

Meares decided to winter in the sound. The weather was extremely cold. The *Nootka* was icebound, scurvy prevailed among the crew, and in the agonizing months ahead 23 members died. Meares wrote of that winter: *"We continued to see and lament a gradual diminution of our crew from this terrible disaster. Too often did I find myself called to assist in performing the dreadful office of dragging the dead bodies across the ice to a shallow sepulcher, which with our own hands we had hewn out for them on the shore. The sledge in which we fetched the wood was their hearse and the chasm in the ice their grave."*

Spring thaw released the *Nootka* and she sailed for the Orient. The following year, 1788, Meares returned to the Northwest coast in command of *Felice Adventurer*. At Nootka canoes filled with natives surrounded the ship. To their astonishment they saw one of their fellow tribesmen, Comekela, standing at attention on the deck wearing a military hat with colorful ribbons and a scarlet regimental coat decorated with polished brass buttons. Comekela had been taken to China by an earlier expedition and a feast of whale blubber was held in honor of his return.

Also aboard the *Felice Adventurer* were Chinese workers and the framework for a schooner. Meares purchased a tract of land from the natives for two pistols and directed his workers first to erect a fort and then to begin cutting timber for a schooner.

While this work progressed Meares and the *Felice Adventurer* ranged south along the coast. On July 6, 1788, they passed the promontory Heceta called Cape St. Roc and a search was begun for the river he had noted in that vicinity.

Meares wrote: *"We now discovered distant land beyond this promontory and we pleased ourselves with the expectation of its being Cape St. Roc of the Spaniards, near which they are said to have found a good port. By half past eleven we doubled the cape, at a distance of three miles, having a clear and perfect view of the shore in every part, on which we did not discern a living creature, or the least trace of habitable life. A prodigious easterly swell rolled on the shore, and the soundings gradually decreased from 40 to 16 fathoms, over a hard sandy bottom. After we had rounded the promontory, a large bay, as we had imagined, opened to our view, that bore a very promising appearance, and into which we steered with every encouraging expectation....As we steered in, the water shoaled to nine, eight and seven fathoms, when breakers were seen from the deck, right ahead, and from the masthead, they were observed to extend across the bay; we therefore hauled out, and directed our course to the opposite shore, to see if there was any channel, or if we could discover any port. The name of Cape Disappointment was given the promontory, and the bay obtained the title of Deception Bay. By an indifferent meridian observation it lies in the latitude of 46 degrees, 10 minutes, north....We can now with safety assert that there is no such river as that of St. Roc exists, as laid down in the Spanish charts...."*

Because of the string of rough breakers and his personal doubt of the accuracy of Spanish charts, Meares missed discovering the *Great River of the West*. He returned to Nootka.

The schooner which had been built during his absence was launched and christened the *North West America*. Except for Russian vessels built much farther north, the *North West America* was the first ship launched in the North Pacific and was intended to be used to run up and down the coast collecting furs for other ships to take to China. Soon after the launching, Meares sailed for China with a cargo of furs.

A number of ships arrived off the North Pacific coast. Most were British running under the flag of the East India Company or the South Sea Company. The ships were all in search of fur and Viceroy Florez of New Spain (Mexico) was annoyed by this flurry of activity, and even more disturbed by the news that Russia was planning to move into the southern latitudes. He considered this a serious intrusion into Spanish domain and ordered Don Estevan Jose' Martinez to lead a military expedition to Nootka. He was to reclaim the land for the King of Spain and build an outpost. Russian and British ships were to be warned they were in violation of Spanish waters and Martinez was given the authority to use what force he deemed necessary.

Martinez and his convoy of warships arrived at Nootka in the spring of 1789 to find three ships at anchor: the *Columbia Rediviva* and *Lady Washington* flying the Stars and Stripes, and the *Iphigenia Nubiana* which, noticing the Spanish ships, promptly ran up a Portuguese flag. The Americans were new as a country, posed no challenge to Spain, and Martinez ignored them. The *Iphigenia*, commanded by Captain William Douglas, an Englishman, was promptly seized and boarded.

On July 3, 1789, the *Argonaut*, a ship financed by Captain Meares and a joint stock company and licensed under the East India Company, sailed into Nootka. It was seized by Martinez. The crew was taken prisoner, placed in irons and shipped south to Viceroy Florez who found himself in a very delicate situation. If Martinez called for reinforcements they could not be provided; his own position as viceroy had been terminated and his successor was on the way, and he had never received confirmation of his initial action of sending warships to the North Pacific.

Meanwhile Martinez seized two more ships, the *North West America* and the *Princess Royal*, both belonging to Meares and his joint stock company. When Captain Meares received word of the seizures he immediately set sail for England and made a convincing appeal before Parliament. Parliament acted just as Meares had hoped. England took a warlike stance, activated her navy, alerted her allies and warned British colonies around the world to prepare defenses.

Spain operated from a position of weakness. Her navy was no longer powerful and her only strong ally, France, was in the throes of a great revolution. She could not be counted on for any aid. The Spanish government yielded and chose a diplomatic solution to war. On October 28, 1790, all differences between the two nations were settled with the signing of the Nootka Convention. This treaty stipulated that all British property seized by the Spanish would be returned. In exchange, Britain agreed none of her ships would trespass within 10 leagues of the coast already occupied by Spain. It was further agreed that each country would give the other access to unsettled land.

The door to the North Pacific was open. The land and its spoils were there for the taking.

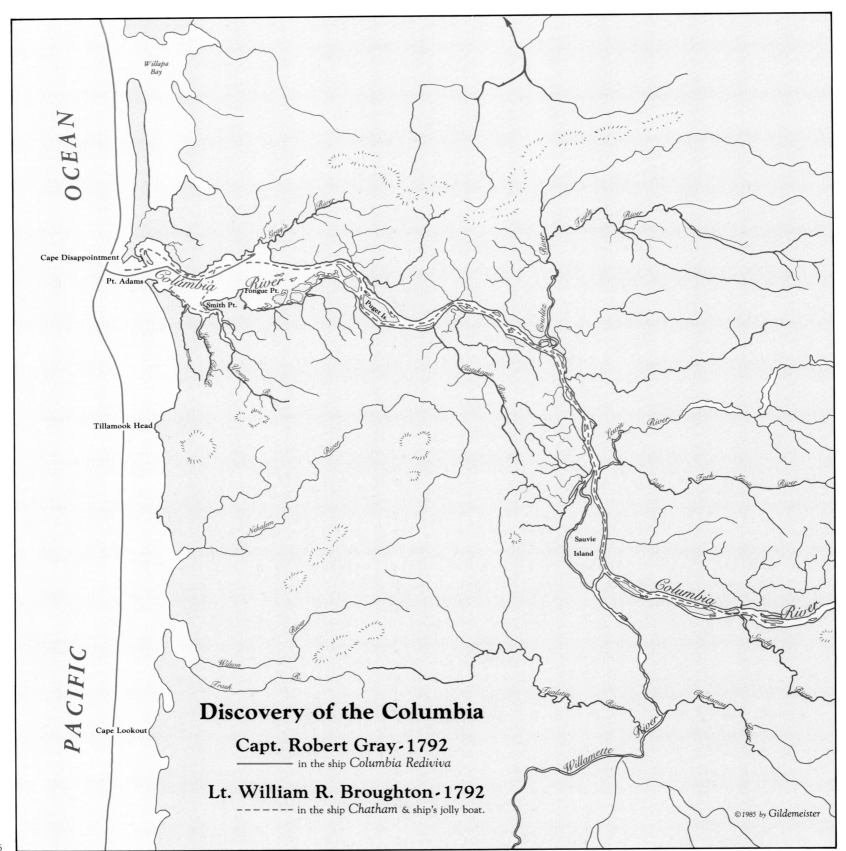

Discovery of the Columbia

Capt. Robert Gray - 1792
——————— in the ship *Columbia Rediviva*

Lt. William R. Broughton - 1792
- - - - - - - in the ship *Chatham* & ship's jolly boat.

©1985 by *Gildemeister*

American Traders

Six American businessmen met one evening in Boston. Their purpose was to form a stock company actively pursuing trade with China. The six invested $50,000 and purchased two vessels: the *Columbia Rediviva*, a full-rigged ship of 212 tons burden, 83 feet long and carrying 10 guns; and the *Lady Washington*, a small sloop of 90 tons. John Kendrick was commissioned to head the expedition, Robert Gray was second in command.

To commemorate launching the enterprise, a medal was struck in the likeness of the two ships. On one side were the words, *Columbia and Washington Commanded by J. Kendrick*; on the other, *Fitted at Boston, N. America for the Pacific Ocean* with the names of the six businessmen and the year 1787.

The *Columbia* and the *Washington* were outfitted with cargo which would appeal to uncivilized hearts: blankets, beads, calicos, knives, tin mirrors, brass buttons and bits of scrap iron. The ships departed with an enthusiastic Boston send-off on October 1, 1787. Emerging from the harbor they squared sails and set a course that would take them around the tip of South America.

During the voyage the ships were separated and Gray, commander of the *Washington*, arrived in the North Pacific first. He put in at what he described as a *"tolerably commodious harbor"*, believed to be Tillamook Bay. The natives appeared friendly and made the visitors presents of berries and freshly-caught crabs. The Americans, beginning to suffer scurvy, gratefully accepted.

After the feast Gray sent a shore party to collect grass to feed the livestock on board. One of them, a lad named Marcos, absentmindedly left his small cutlass sticking in sand near a clump of grass. He turned back to get it, but one of the natives lurking nearby grabbed it first. Marcos made a rush for the Indian. There was a short struggle. Marcos fell dead and the Indian ran away.

Swords flashed. A musket fired. A native pitched forward on his face. There were more shots and several more natives went down. The landing party retreated and rowed back to the ship where Gray ordered abandonment of the harbor.

The *Washington* arrived at Nootka Sound on August 16, 1788, and was welcomed by Captain Meares and Captain Douglas. A week later the *Columbia* limped into port, three of her crew dead from scurvy.

The American ships were at anchor during the confrontation between Martinez's Spanish warships and the British traders. Kendrick and Gray refused to become involved in the matter. They took turns running the *Washington* up and down the coast collecting furs and transferring them to the *Columbia* which maintained her position in the sound.

For unknown reasons Kendrick and Gray switched commands. Kendrick took command of the *Washington* and remained on the coast while Gray sailed the *Columbia* to Canton and on to her home port. The *Columbia* arrived in Boston with a cargo of tea, becoming the first ship to circle the world flying the Stars and Stripes. But the inflated profits the promoters had hoped for were not realized. The scarcity of tea during and after the Revolutionary War had been alleviated by other merchants. Some partners wanted out. Their interest was purchased by the others and $25,000 was raised toward a second trade expedition.

The *Columbia* was outfitted with 135 barrels of beef, 60 barrels of pork, 1,500 pounds of gunpowder and 5 hogshead of New England and West Indian rum. The cargo included those items most cherished by the natives — scrap metal, copper sheets, scarlet material, knives and buttons.

Columbia's second voyage began September 28, 1790. She reached the North Pacific the following June. Gray fully expected to find Kendrick and the *Washington* on the coast, but the ship had slipped off to the Sandwich Islands. It was there, at Karakakooa Bay, that Kendrick was accidently struck and killed by grapeshot fired from a British vessel saluting him.

The *Columbia* spent the winter of 1791-1792 in the harbor of Clayoquot near Nootka. Quarters were built on an easily-defended strip of land and fortified against the possibility of attack. Gray and his crew attempted to cultivate friendly relations, but the natives seemed particularly unfriendly that season. They allowed only one member of the crew to associate with them, a native passenger taken aboard in the Sandwich Islands on the first voyage. His name was Attoo.

The natives promised to make Attoo chief over all their tribes if he would betray the Americans. They wanted him to smuggle them gunpowder and wet the gunpowder remaining at the fort so it would be useless. The chance of being a great chief was tantalizing, but Attoo acted honorably and informed Captain Gray. The *Columbia* had been pulled from the water for the winter but Gray ordered her quickly refloated and her guns remounted. The natives witnessed this, knew they had lost the element of surprise and made exaggerated overtures of friendship.

In the spring of 1792 Gray abandoned the fort and sailed the *Columbia* south, following close to the coastline and mapping the lay of the land. Near the 46th parallel Gray recognized signs of a great river, a darkness to the water and evidence of debris washed from inland. He searched for the source, but the river eluded him and at length the *Columbia* sailed north.

With the break of a rosy dawn on April 29, the *Columbia* watch called out that a ship was on the horizon. As it drew nearer Gray ran up the Stars and Stripes and fired a gun to leeward. Within a few hours Captain George Vancouver aboard the *Discovery* was within hailing distance.

Vancouver had been on the North Pacific before, in 1778, as a midshipman with Captain Cook. He was here now carrying out an official mission for the British government — to survey and map the Pacific coast from the latitude 30 degrees to 60 degrees, north.

Vancouver mapped the coastline on the way up and told Gray that, though he had searched for the river in the latitude reported by Heceta, he had found no evidence it existed. *"Under the most favorable circumstances of wind and weather I have found the whole coast to be one compact and nearly straight barrier against the sea,"* he said.

Gray volunteered information that he had been off the mouth of a great river in the latitude of 46 degrees, 10 minutes — precisely where Heceta had located it — and found the bar impassable for the nine days he was there. Vancouver refused to believe Gray. He had surveyed the area and found nothing to suggest a great river emptied there. The two ships parted. The *Discovery* sailed north into the Strait of Juan de Fuca and the *Columbia* sailed south to its destiny with discovery.

On May 7 an opening along the shore was noted, explored and named Bulfinch Harbor after one of the ship's owners, but the officers and crew referred to it as Gray's Harbor. Lying at anchor in this harbor late on a moonlit night, the ship's watch spotted several canoes launch. Captain Gray ordered all hands to stand by. When it was evident the warriors in the canoes were making directly for the ship he ordered a round of musket fire over their heads. This action forced the attackers to veer away, but soon they were making another run at the ship. This time one of the *Columbia's* cannons blew a canoe and at least 20 warriors out of the water.

In the morning a congregation of natives paddled out to the *Columbia*. Trade resumed as if the previous night's tragedy had never occurred. The *Columbia* remained in the harbor until the evening of the 10th when she weighed anchor and stood down the bay. At eight o'clock she emerged from between the heads of the dimly-lit capes at the entrance and crossed into the ocean. Gray ordered the main top gallant yard sent up and set all sail. There would be no further delay in locating the *Great River of the West* and crossing over its bar.

The *Columbia's* log notes on May 11: *"At 4 A.M. saw the entrance of our desired port bearing east-southeast, distance six leagues."* The wind blew strong out of the west. Breakers beat the shore and no opening appeared visible. The water was discolored an inky brown, a mix of inland soils carried by the flooding current of a great river. The *Columbia* was positioned out past the breakers, poised at the brink of discovery.

Gray carefully searched the bar trying to locate the safest point to cross. At last he gave the order to set sail. According to Gray's log: "At 8 A.M., *being a little to windward of the entrance to the harbor, bore away, and run in east-northeast, between breakers, having from five to seven fathoms of water. When we were over the bar we found this to be a large river of fresh water, up which we steered. Many canoes came alongside. At 1 P.M. came to with the small bower, in two fathoms, black and white sand. The entrance between the bars bore west-southwest, distant ten miles. The north side of the river a half-mile distant from the ship; the south side of the same, two and a half miles distance; a village on the north side of the river west by north, distant three-quarters of a mile. Vast numbers of natives came alongside. People employed in pumping the salt water out of our water casks, in order to fill with fresh, while the ship floated in. So ends.*"

The *Great River of the West* had been discovered. Later this achievement would be of major importance to the United States' claim to the Pacific Northwest. The American captain who dared the breakers, knowing his ship could have been dashed on a sunken reef and swallowed by the sea in this far-distant corner of the world, named this river in honor of his valiant ship, *Columbia's River.*

One of *Columbia's* seamen, 17-year-old John Boit, wrote in his journal: "*The river extended to the N.E. as far as eye cou'd reach, and water fit to drink as far down as the Bars, at the entrance. We directed our course up this noble River in search of a village. The beach was lin'd with natives who ran along the shore following the ship. Soon after, above 20 canoes came off, and brought a good lot of furs and salmon, which last they sold two for a board Nail. The furs we likewise bought cheap, for Copper and Cloth. They appear'd to view the Ship with the great astonishment and no doubt we was the first civilized people that they ever saw....*

"*We lay in this place till the 20th May, during which time we put the ship in good order and fill'd up all the water casks along side, it being very good. These Natives talk'd the same language as those farther South, but we cou'd not learn it. Observ'd that the canoes that came from down river, brought no otter skins, and I believe the otter constantly keeps in salt water. They however always came well stocked with land furs, and capital salmon. The tide set down the whole time and was rapid. Whole trees sometimes came down with the stream. The Indians inform'd us there was 50 villages on the banks of this river.*

"*On the 15th we took up the anchor, and stood up river, but soon found the water to be shoal so that the ship took the ground, after proceeding 7 or 8 miles from our first station. However soon got off again. Sent the Cutter and found the main Channel was on the South side, and that there was a sand bank in the middle. As we did not expect to procure Otter furs at any distance from the Sea, we contented ourselves in our present situation, which was a very pleasant one. I landed abreast the ship with Capt. Gray to view the country and take possession, leaving charge with the 2d Officer. Found much clear ground, fit for cultivation, and the woods mostly clear from underbrush. None of the Natives came near us.*

"*May 18. Shifted the Ship's berth to her old station abreast the Village Chinoak, command'd by a chief Polack. Vast many canoes, full of Indians, from different parts of the River were constantly alongside. Capt. Gray named this river Columbia's and the North entrance Cape Hancock, and the South Point, Adams.*"

While on the river the crew caulked the pinnace, repaired and painted the *Columbia* and traded with the natives. May 20 the weather was pleasant with a light breeze and the *Columbia* made ready to sail in the afternoon. Full tide was at one o'clock and the *Columbia* went with it, but at two o'clock, upon nearing the bar, the wind failed. Without wind she could never run the bar and if she drifted in the breakers, she would likely be torn apart. The ship was brought up in three and one-half fathoms of water with the draw of the current and tide running at five knots. Later a fresh wind sprang from the sea and Gray wrote in his log: "At 5 P.M. *we were out, clear of all bars, and in twenty fathoms of water. A breeze came from the southward; we bore away to the northward, set all sail to the best advantage.*"

After claiming Columbia's River for the United States of America, Gray sailed north to Queen Charlotte's Isles. There the *Columbia* ran aground on a hidden rock and was nearly lost when the tide went out and left her on her side. On the incoming tide she was successfully freed but leaked badly. Kept afloat by the crew laboring on the pumps, she limped into Nootka and was beached for repairs.

Exploring the Columbia

Informed of Gray's discovery, Captain Vancouver lost no time verifying the American's claim. His ship *Discovery* and the *Chatham*, a small brig, arrived at the mouth of the Columbia River October 19, 1792. The following morning Vancouver wrote in his log: *"The morning was calm and fair, yet the heavy cross swell continued...the breakers seemed to extend without the least interruption from shore to shore....*

"The flood at one o'clock running in our favor, we weighed with a signal as before for the Chatham to lead. With boats sounding ahead we made all sail to windward in four to six fathoms of water. The Chatham being further advanced in the channel, and having more wind and tide, made a greater progress than did the Discovery."

The *Chatham* cleared the bar, stood inside the line of breakers and a hearty cheer went up from her crew. At the last moment Vancouver lost his nerve for the crossing. He wrote: *"...the ebb making strongly against us, with scarcely sufficient wind to command the ship, we were driven out of the channel into 13 fathoms water, where we anchored for the night; the serenity of which flattered us with the hope of getting in the next day.*

"The clearness of the atmosphere enabled us to see the high round snowy mountain....This I have distinguished by the name of Mount St. Helens, in honor of his Britannic Majesty's ambassador at the court of Madrid.

"Sunday, 21. All hope of getting into Columbia river vanished on Sunday morning which brought with it a fresh gale from the S.E., and every appearance of approaching bad weather, which the falling of the mercury in the barometer also indicated. We therefore weighed and stood out to sea."

The *Discovery*, sails billowing, made south to Monterey Bay on the coast of California. Lieutenant W. R. Broughton, commander of the *Chatham*, was left at the mouth of the great, unexplored river.

The *Chatham* sailed upriver. Broughton sighted and named Tongue Point and entered a large bay he named Young's Bay in honor of Sir George Young of the Royal Navy. He then undertook, with the ship's boat and a crew of oarsmen, an exploration, and as they made their way against the current a large number of natives in canoes followed at a short distance.

Broughton applied names to landmarks as they came near them: Puget Island named in honor of the lieutenant on the *Discovery*, Walker's Island named after the *Chatham's* surgeon and Coffin Mountain named for the burial ground near the water's edge where the native dead were laid to rest on raised platforms.

On a point of land, at the confluence of a tributary he named River Mannings (Willamette River), Broughton made note in his journal: *"A very distant high snowy mountain now appeared rising beautifully conspicuous in the midst of an extensive tract of low, or moderately elevated land lying S.67E. and seemed to announce the termination of the river."*

The expedition continued and the current of the Columbia flowed faster, sometimes running in short, turbulent rapids that made rowing difficult. At one point, on a sandy bank Broughton named Point Vancouver, he went ashore and despite Gray's prior claim he took possession of the Columbia River and all it drained for the Crown.

On the evening of the seventh day they landed on the north shore opposite Baring's River (Sandy River). Here in the light of a fresh moon, the majestic mountain that had dominated the eastern sky for several days was named Mt. Hood after Lord Hood, a member of the Board of Admiralty under the Earl of Chatham.

At this camp, in the light of a driftwood fire an old Indian chief, who had been acting as guide, attempted to communicate what the river above was like. He repeatedly pointed at the silhouette of Mt. Hood, shining in the moonlight under a fresh dusting of snow, to indicate direction and scooped water in his hands and poured it out to suggest waterfalls and dangerous rapids.

Broughton stood by the fire listening to night sounds along the river. He knew from coming this close to the mountain and from observing the high water mark that the Columbia River originated much farther inland. The expedition had only three days rations remaining. He decided they would go no farther; they would return to the *Chatham.*

The old chief stayed with the expedition until it neared the mouth of River Mannings. Then his canoe turned away. Broughton had taken a deep liking to the chief, and to a side channel of the Columbia he applied the name Friendly Reach and to the landmark where the chief was last seen, the name Parting Point.

Broughton and the crew returned to the *Chatham;* sail was spread and the ship proceeded to the mouth of the river and out over the bar to the prearranged rendezvous with Captain Vancouver at Monterey Bay.

Columbia River Sunset

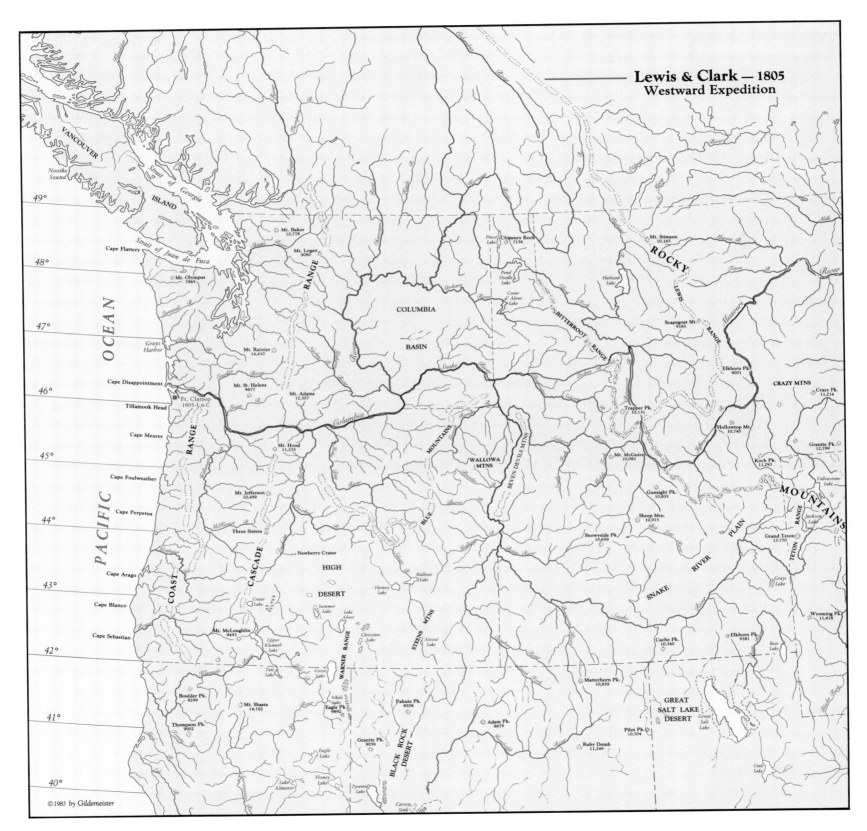

Lewis & Clark — 1805
Westward Expedition

VANCOUVER
ISLAND

Nootka Sound

Strait of Georgia

Strait of Juan de Fuca

Cape Flattery

OCEAN

Mt. Olympus
7965

Grays Harbor

PACIFIC

Cape Disappointment

Tillamook Head

Cape Meares

Cape Foulweather

Cape Perpetua

Cape Arago

Cape Blanco

Cape Sebastian

Ft. Clatsop
1805-L&C

RANGE

COAST

RANGE

Mt. Baker
10,778

Mt. Logan
9080

RANGE

Mt. Rainier
14,410

Mt. St. Helens
9677

Mt. Adams
12,307

Mt. Hood
11,235

Mt. Jefferson
10,499

Three Sisters

CASCADE

Newberry Crater

Crater Lake

Mt. McLoughlin
9493

COLUMBIA

BASIN

Columbia

Snake

Chimney Rock
7136

Priest Lake

Pend Oreille Lake

Coeur d'Alene Lake

BITTERROOT RANGE

ROCKY

Mt. Stimson
10,165

Scapegoat Mt.
9185

Flathead Lake

LEWIS RANGE

Missouri

Elkhorn Pk.
9001

CRAZY MTNS

Crazy Pk.
11,214

Trapper Pk.
10,131

Hollowtop Mt.
10,740

Granite Pk.
12,799

Mt. McGuire
10,082

Koch Pk.
11,293

MOUNTAINS

SEVEN DEVILS MTNS

WALLOWA
MTNS

MOUNTAINS

BLUE

Gunsight Pk.
10,835

Sheep Mtn.
10,915

Snowyside Pk.
10,659

Grand Teton
13,770

Yellowstone Lake

Jackson Lake

TETON RANGE

RIVER

SNAKE

PLAIN

Wyoming Pk.
11,418

HIGH

DESERT

Harney Lake

Malheur Lake

STEENS MTNS

Alvord Lake

Summer Lake

Lake Abert

Christmas Lake

Upper Klamath Lake

WARNER RANGE

Goose Lake

Tule Lake

Snake

Cache Pk.
10,340

Elkhorn Pk.
9381

Bear Lake

GREAT
SALT LAKE
DESERT

Great Salt Lake

Matterhorn Pk.
10,839

Pilot Pk.
10,704

Ruby Dome
11,349

Boulder Pk.
8299

Mt. Shasta
14,162

Thompson Pk.
9002

Eagle Pk.
9892

Granite Pk.
9056

Eagle Lake

Honey Lake

Lake Almanor

Pyramid Lake

Pahute Pk.
8508

Adam Pk.
8679

BLACK ROCK
DESERT

Carson Sink

Utah Lake

49°
48°
47°
46°
45°
44°
43°
42°
41°
40°

© 1985 by Gildemeister

Overland Exploration

The stormy waters of the North Pacific had been sailed and the most prominent landmarks named, but the interior was a void, an unknown enriched by vague legends, imaginary wonders of nature and said to be populated by strange tribes of savage Indians.

Along the civilized east coast of the continent were constant whispers about the interior, about a great river that drained much of the interior and emptied into the Pacific Ocean. The first in search of this fabled river was Pierre Gaultier de Varennes de la Verendrye. A trader and explorer, Varennes was commissioned by France in 1728 and directed by the colonial government at Montreal to undertake an exploration and push the limits of French trade as far west as possible.

Varennes reached a point where he beheld an uninterrupted string of lofty mountains to the west which he named the Shining Mountains (Rocky Mountains). Indians in the vicinity told him of a mighty river that flowed west from the mountains, but Varennes turned back rather than attempt the rugged crossing.

Twenty-five years later a French writer, Le Page du Pratz, published a fictional story about an Indian who ascended the Missouri River to its source in the Shining Mountains. He crossed this high and dangerous mountain chain and beheld a beautiful river that flowed to the ocean. Reaching the ocean, the narrator of the epic said, *"I was so delighted I could not speak. My eyes were too small for my soul's ease. The wind so disturbed the great water, that I thought the blows it gave would beat the land to pieces."*

Subsequent maps of North America, based on Le Page's fiction, laid down a river flowing from the Shining Mountains to the Pacific and named it the *Great River of the West*.

The name Oregon probably had its origin in the Indian language. The first white man's use of the word *Ouragon* was by Major Robert Rogers. The English army officer submitted to King George III a proposal August 1765 to take an expeditionary force of 200 men on an overland search for the Northwest Passage. The route detailed was *"from the Great Lakes towards the Head of the Mississippi, and from thence to the River called by the Indians Ouragon, which flows into the Pacific Ocean...."*

The proposal was rejected. Instead of searching for the Northwest Passage, Major Rogers was appointed governor-commandant of Fort Mackinac at the head of Lake Michigan. His service began in August 1766 and one of his first actions was to outfit an expedition to locate the Northwest Passage.

Mapmaker for this expedition was Jonathan Carver, a native of Connecticut. Although the expedition was unsuccessful, Carver published a book in 1778 titled, **Travels Through the Interior Parts of North America**. In the introduction Carver penned these words: *"...four great rivers take their rise within a few leagues of each other, nearly about the center of this great continent; The River Bourbon which empties into Hudson's Bay; the Waters of Saint Lawrence; The Mississippi; and the River Oregon, or the River of the West...."*

The word Oregon was not popularized for another three decades — not until American poet William Cullen Bryant penned the immortal verse in his classical masterpiece, *"Thanatopsis"*:

Where rolls the Oregon and hears no sound
Save his own dashings — yet the dead are there!

Alexander Mackenzie

King Charles II of England in 1670 issued a charter to The Company of Adventurers of England Trading into Hudson Bay, afterwards known as the Hudson's Bay Company. This charter provided the Company with the authorization to explore and trade in all the region draining into Hudson Bay. But the Company did little to build an empire until after the Seven Years' War ended French domination of Canada. For two decades after, the Company held a fur trading monopoly, but in 1783 another British fur company, the North West Company, was organized in Montreal and became a fierce and bitter competitor to the Hudson's Bay Company.

Alexander Mackenzie, a partner in the North West Company, was one of the most enterprising and venturesome explorers of the fur trading era. He was in charge of the outpost at Fort Chipewyan near the southwest end of Lake Athabasca and wondered whether the discharge of Lake Athabasca flowed into the Arctic Ocean or back into Hudson Bay. In summer 1789, with a small party in three bark canoes, Mackenzie descended the Slave River to Great Slave Lake and took the discharge river which bears his name. He ran it to its mouth in the Arctic Ocean. This exploration determined once and for all that there could be no Northwest Passage across the American continent.

With this successful exploration of the country to the north, Mackenzie was of the opinion he could be the first to travel overland to the Pacific. On October 10, 1792, Mackenzie left Fort Chipewyan with ten well-seasoned men. They ascended Peace River and wintered in the Rocky Mountains. Late in the spring they started for the summit carrying a canoe, provisions and trade goods.

By the middle of June they had crossed over the top and found a river of considerable flow, the Tacoutche Tesse (Fraser River). Mackenzie concluded this must be the *River of the West*, but after following it 250 miles and finding the canyon through which it flowed becoming more narrow and the stream obstructed by boulders and rapids, he resolved to strike overland due west for the coast.

They came out at the mouth of the Bella Coola River in the latitude of 52 degrees. Mackenzie mixed some vermillion and animal grease and inscribed on the face of a large rock that faced the Pacific Ocean: *Alexander Mackenzie from Canada by land, the 22nd day of July 1793.*

Returning to civilization Mackenzie published in London a detailed account of the first overland crossing of the North American continent. It helped serve British interests and established a strong claim to all of the interior lying south of the Russian possessions. For his service to the Crown Mackenzie was knighted by the King of England.

Lewis and Clark

The year after Captain Gray sailed through the breakers and into the Columbia River a French botanist, Andre' Michaux, proposed to the American Philosophical Society that he lead an overland expedition to the Pacific Ocean. The Society opened a subscription list that included George Washington who gave $25, and Thomas Jefferson and Alexander Hamilton who donated $12.50 each. A young army officer named Meriwether Lewis was chosen to accompany Michaux.

The two started west but were overtaken in Kentucky by a messenger. He presented Michaux with a letter from the French Minister of the Interior directing him to pursue his studies of plants and trees in regions less remote. The expedition was abandoned.

After Thomas Jefferson was elected the third president of the United States in 1800 he appointed Meriwether Lewis his private secretary. The President wished the western frontier explored and his secretary, an ardent explorer, made plans to form an expedition. The President penned a confidential message to the Congress suggesting a small group be outfitted and sent into the country west of the Mississippi: *"...an intelligent officer, with ten or twelve chosen men, fit for the enterprise and willing to undertake it...might explore the whole line, even to the Western Ocean....While other civilized nations have encountered great expense to enlarge the boundaries of knowledge, by undertaking voyages of discovery, and for other literary purposes, in various parts and directions, our nation seems to owe to the same object, as well as to its own interests, to explore this the only line of easy communication across the continent, and so directly traversing our own port of it...."*

An appropriation of $2,500 was readily voted by the Congress. As preparations for outfitting an expedition began, President Jefferson received news that Spain had transferred possession of vast Louisiana to France. He was greatly alarmed. Settlers from the States had been taking up residence in the Ohio and Mississippi river valleys in increasing numbers and they relied on the rivers for commerce. The President conferred with the Congress and sent a special envoy to Paris to negotiate with Napoleon for the purchase of New Orleans and the mouth of the Mississippi. But Napoleon needed capital to finance his war more than he needed a large territory on the North American continent. He surprised the Americans by proposing to sell the entire Louisiana territory for $15,000,000 — a proposal quickly accepted. The United States doubled its territory without a drop of blood, and even more significance was given to the expedition being formed.

Meriwether Lewis was a 30-year-old native of Charlottesville, Virginia, the son of prominent Revolutionary War figures. His father died while Meriwether was very young and the boy grew up in the out-of-doors, hunted opossum with hounds at night by age eight and at eighteen was successfully managing his mother's plantation.

He joined the army and rose rapidly in the ranks until President Jefferson asked him to act as his private secretary. The salary was $500 a year, with board and lodging at the executive mansion. President Jefferson described Lewis as the obvious choice to lead the expedition of the Louisiana Purchase and the Pacific coast because Lewis was *"brave, prudent, habituated to the woods, & familiar with Indian manners and character. He is not regularly educated, but he possesses a great mass of accurate observation on all subjects of nature...."*

Lewis felt responsibility for the expedition should be shared and requested that a friend and army mate, William Clark, be appointed as co-commander. President Jefferson agreed.

William Clark was 33 years old, the ninth child of a Kentucky frontier family. He joined the army at age 19 and met Meriwether Lewis while fighting the Indian wars. After serving five years Clark returned to Kentucky where he remained until receiving Lewis's letter, written June 19, 1803, asking him to become a member of the expedition. Lewis and Clark were given joint command. Lewis was to head the scientific phases of the work and Clark the military.

President Jefferson prepared the instructions for the expedition, noting the objective was *"to explore the Missouri River, and such principal streams of it, as by its course and communication with the waters of the Pacific Ocean, whether the Columbia, Oregon, Colorado or any other river named, may offer the most direct and practicable water communication across the continent, for the purposes of commerce."* An accurate journal was to be kept and the Indian tribes, their language, traditions and customs were to be noted. The general character of the country was to be observed; the soil, minerals and plants of the regions visited were to be catalogued and climatic conditions noted.

Regarding the Indians President Jefferson directed: *"In all your intercourse with the natives treat them in the most friendly and conciliatory manner which their own conduct will admit; allay all jealousies as to the object of your journey; satisfy them of its innocence...."*

By the spring of 1804 a company of men including Lewis and Clark, four sergeants, twenty private soldiers, eleven voyageurs and nine frontiersmen were assembled near the outpost town of St. Louis. They departed on the 4th day of May. Some of the men moved a band of horses along the bank while the others rowed boats up the Missouri River. They planned to use the boats to the headwaters and from there cross over the Rockies on horseback.

The men lived off the country, shooting game at every opportunity and sending out hunting parties. The journey up the Missouri was slow. The current was swift and there were sandbars and deadheads concealed just below the surface. At first the Indians they encountered were unfriendly because of past experience with the white man, but the farther they traveled the more hospitable the Indians became.

In September, 1,600 miles from St. Louis, the party reached the land of the Arikaras Indians who supplied them with corn, beans and squash. Seasons were changing and it was decided winter quarters should be selected. They chose a site beside the village of the Mandan tribe. The men felled timber and erected a triangular stockade with barracks along two walls.

At the Mandan village they found a French-Canadian, a former Northwester, Toussaint Charboneau, who could understand and speak the Indian languages. Charboneau was married to a Shoshone Indian, Sacajawea. She had been captured by a hostile war party as a young girl, brought east of the Rocky Mountains and kept as a slave. Charboneau purchased Sacajawea from her captors.

It was arranged for Charboneau and Sacajawea to leave with the expedition in the spring as translators. A tolerable winter was passed with plenty of buffalo, deer and elk to eat. On February 11 Sacajawea gave birth to a son. On April 7, 1805, with the addition of Charboneau, his wife and child, the expedition departed the Mandan village.

Near the end of April the company reached a river Charboneau called Roche Jaune and which the Americans named the Yellowstone. While camped here Lewis wrote in his journal of the grizzly bear: *"Of the strength and ferocity of this animal the indians had given us dreadful accounts; they never attack him but in parties of six or eight persons, and even then are often defeated, with the loss of one or more of the party. Having no weapons but bows and arrows, and the bad guns with which the traders supply them, they are obliged to approach very near to the bear; and as no wound except through the head or heart is mortal, they frequently fall a sacrifice if they miss their aim. He rather attacks than avoids a man, and such is the terror which he has inspired that the indians who go in quest of him paint themselves and perform all the superstitious rites customary when they make war on a neighboring nation."*

Lewis had his first encounter with a grizzly in the company of a hunter. They came upon two bears, each man fired and each wounded a bear. One bear ran away but the other charged Lewis and chased him 80 yards before he could get his rifle reloaded. He shot the bear from point blank range but failed to stop the brute. Finally a third shot, fired by the other hunter, killed it.

A month later, near Great Falls on the Missouri, Lewis shot a buffalo and went to work dressing the animal, forgetting to reload. When he looked up there was a grizzly twenty yards away coming at him. His first instinct was to raise his rifle, but just as quickly he remembered not reloading. He looked around. There was not a tree nor bush within 300 yards. He tried to back away and leave the buffalo for the bear, but the grizzly raised up, growled ferociously and charged. Lewis ran. At the edge of the river he dove off a high bank and into the water. The bear stopped, wheeled around and ambled off.

As the company followed the Missouri into the Rocky Mountains its flow continually diminished until at last Lewis wrote in his journal: "…*the stream gradually became smaller, till after going two miles farther it had diminished in width that one of the men in a fit of enthusiasm, with one foot on each side of the river, thanked God that he had lived to bestride the Missouri….*"

Lewis and two hunters went ahead of the main party. They crossed the Continental Divide and for several weeks found scarcely enough game to sustain themselves, though they saw sign. They saw no Indians until the afternoon of August 13 when they came upon two women, a man and some dogs on a hillside about a mile away. Lewis set down his pack and, so not to call alarm, proceeded alone, waving a small flag as a sign of peace. The Indians allowed him to come halfway and then the women ran off. The man stayed until Lewis was within 100 yards and then he followed the women into the underbrush. Only the barking dogs remained. Lewis tried to work his way close to one of them so he might tie trinkets around its neck to show friendly intentions, but was unsuccessful.

Lewis called up his men and they overtook the Indians in two miles. The women bowed their heads to the ground in submission but Lewis raised the first one onto her feet and presented her with a number of small trinkets.

The Indians were from a band of the Shoshone nation. They took Lewis and his men to their village and Lewis attempted to purchase horses to take back to the main party struggling over the mountains. The Indians were reluctant to sell until Lewis made known a Shoshone woman was accompanying the others.

The meeting of Sacajawea and her people was a dramatic and emotional scene. She was recognized as the girl who had been captured many years before and she recognized the chief as her brother Cameahwait. From him she learned that her family, except for another brother who was away, was dead.

With this relationship established, the Indians sold the Americans 29 horses for six dollars worth of trinkets and agreed to guide the expedition through the mountains to the Bitterroot River (Clark's Fork). From there the Indians returned to their homeland and the expedition continued to the territory of the Pierced nose Indians (Nez Perce) where they were given a feast of buffalo meat, dried salmon berries and several kinds of roots.

Reaching the Kos-kos-kee (Clearwater River), the company felled cedar trees and fashioned dugout canoes. The horses were left in the safekeeping of the Indians and the expedition continued by water down the Kos-kos-kee to Lewis River (Snake River). With little game and few fish because of the late season, the white men purchased dogs from the Indians for food. This disgusted the Indians who ate dog meat as a last resort, but the company men found the meat, if well-cooked, quite palatable.

Snake River Canyon

They reached the confluence with the Columbia by mid-October and shortly after observed a mountain far to the west the Indians called Tumtum (Mt. Hood). The day the mountain was spotted Clark walked along the bank hunting and shot a crane on the wing. The Indians of a nearby village were greatly alarmed at the crack of the rifle. They had never heard one before. They saw the crane fall from the sky and then saw the white man. They believed he was the crane reincarnated and were terrified.

Clark called to them, soothed their fear until they were encouraged to sit with him to smoke a pipe of peace. Clark used the sun glass he carried in his pocket to light his pipe and the natives oohed and aahed at this display of power. They were convinced Clark was a god until the main party arrived and Sacajawea explained that the white men came from the land far to the east.

The canoes passed the mouth of a river the Indians called Towornehiooks (Deschutes) October 22. The speed of the current noticeably increased as the Columbia dropped through a series of rapids leading to what the Indians called Tum, meaning *Sound of Falling Water*. Lewis and Clark named it Great Falls (Celilo Falls). Clark described the river above as confined *"in a narrow channel of about 45 yards...in those narrows the water was agitated in a most shocking manner boils swells & whorlpools, we passed with great risque It being impossible to make a portage of the canoes...."*

Captains Rock on the Columbia Plain

A great number of Indians gathered on the rocky cliffs to watch the canoes make the run through the rapids. The canoes were portaged around the falls and returned to the water. Clark described the Indians found along the river: *"Their noses are all Pierced and the[y] wear a white shell maney of which are 2 Inches long pushed thro' the nose. all the women have flat heads pressed to almost a point at top. The[y] press the female childrens heads between 2 bords when young untill they form the skul as they wish it which is generally verry flat. This amongst those people is considered a great mark of buty, and is practiced in all the tribes we have passed on this river more or less."*

At the Great Shute (Cascade Rapids), supplies and trade goods were portaged and the canoes lowered by sliding them over the rocks on poles placed along the edge of the water. They camped at the bottom of this string of rapids and noticed that the river was affected by the tide. Their spirits were lifted but in the days ahead they were met by wind funneling between the perpendicular basalt cliffs of the gorge. Rock formations took turns appearing and disappearing in the swirling fog and it rained with dreary steadiness.

Passing a large rock on the north side of the river Clark described it as *"a remarkable high rick about 800 feet high & 400 yds round, the Beaten Rock [Beacon Rock]."* And on the 5th of November he complained that *"I could not sleep for the noise kept by the Swans, Geese, White & black brants Duck on a opposite base, & sand hill Crane, they were emencly numerous and their nosie horrid."*

Beacon Rock on the Columbia River

Clark described the valley of the lower Columbia as *"60 miles wide on a Derect line, & extends a great Distance to the right & left, rich thickly covered with tall timber, with a fiew Small Praries bordering on the river and on the Islands; Some fiew standing Ponds & Several Small Streams of running water on either Side of the river; This is certainly a fertill and a handsom valley, at this time crouded with Indians."*

On November 7 Clark wrote: *"Great joy in camp we are in view of the Ocian, (in the morning when fog cleared off just below the last village) this great Pacific Octean which we been so long anxious to See. and the roreing or noise made by the waves brakeing on the rockey Shores (as I suppose) may be heard distictly"*

Because of strong winds and continuous rain, the company was forced to establish an unsatisfactory camp where they were held stormbound for nearly three weeks. It was the plan to make winter quarters near the sea in order to renew their supply of salt. They also hoped to meet a trading vessel from which they could purchase supplies and a stock of trinkets to use for trading on the return trip.

The storm abated enough to allow moving camp to a *"very remarkable knob of land"* projecting into the river (Tongue Point) and here they were stormbound again for ten days.

On December 7 the storm slackened, allowing them to take to the canoes and reach a broad-sweeping blue bay they named Meriwether Bay (Youngs Bay). Thirty feet back from the high tide mark, beside a stream named Lewis and Clark River, Clark scratched the plans for Fort Clatsop in soft sand. It would be 50 feet square with an outer wall of logs. Inside, two barracks would be built to protect them from the elements.

While Fort Clatsop was under construction a party was sent to the seashore to start a salt-boiling operation which produced three quarts of salt a day. Time passed. It rained, snowed and rained again.

Ft. Clatsop

In early January, during a break between storms, a group of Indians visited Fort Clatsop and reported a large whale stranded on the beach to the south. Before Clark could leave to visit the spot Charboneau and Sacajawea begged to be allowed to come along. Clark's journal states: *"The last evening Shabono and his Indian woman was very impatient to be permitted to go with me, and was therefore indulged; She observed that She had traveled a long way with us to See the great water, and that now that monstrous fish was also to be Seen She thought it verry hard that She could not be permitted to See either (She had never yet been to the Ocian)."*

Clark led the party southwest and from a high point of ground overlooking the ocean he noted: *"...from this point I beheld the grandest and most pleasing prospects which my eyes ever surveyed, in my frount a boundless Ocean; to the N. and N.E. the coast as far as my sight could be extended, the Seas rageing with emence wave and brakeing with great force from the rocks of Cape Disapointment as far as I could See...."* This spot was named Clark's Point of View (Tillamook Head).

Clark continued: *"Wind hard from the S.E. and See looked (wild) in the after part of the Day breaking with great force against the Scattering rocks at some distance from Shore, and the ruged rockey points under which we wer obleged to pass and if we had unfortunately made one false Step we Should eneviateably have fallen into the Sea and dashed against the rocks in an instant...and proceeded to the place the whale had perished, found only the Skelleton of this Monster on the Sand between (2 of) the Villages of the Kil a mox nation; the Whale was already pillaged of every Valuable part by the Kilamox Ind. in the Vecinity of whose village's it lay on the Strand where the waves and tide had driven up & left it. this Skeleton measured 105 feet."*

Haystack Rock at Cannon Beach

The winter slowly passed, punctuated by high wind and rain from storm after storm. Only six clear days were mentioned in the journals and only twelve without rain. The men suffered from rheumatism and influenza. Lewis wrote in his journal on March 2, 1806: *"The diet of the sick is so inferior that they recover their strength but slowly. none of them are now sick but all in a state of convalessence with keen appetites and nothing to eat except lean Elk meat."*

The third week of March the company readied itself for the homeward leg of the expedition. On the 23rd they turned their backs to the Pacific. Lewis wrote: *"at 1 P.M. we bid a final adieu to Fort Clatsop...."* And Clark wrote: *"...we loaded our canoes & at 1 P.M. left Fort Clatsop on our homeward bound journey. at this place we had winterd and remain from 7th. of Dec. 1805 to this day* [March 23rd, 1806] *and have lived as well as we had any right to expect, and we can say that we were never one day without three meals of some kind a day either pore Elk meat or roots...."*

Elk at Ft. Clatsop

They paddled upriver twelve days before Indians informed them they had missed the mouth of a great river, the Multnomah (Willamette). From Clark's journal: *"it appeared that this river which they called Mult-no-mah discharged itself behind the Island...we had never seen it."*

Clark, with six men and an Indian guide, set out in a large canoe, backtracking to locate the mouth of a river partially hidden from view by an island the expedition had named Wap-pa-to Island (Sauvie Island). On the back side of the island was a large Indian village. Clark wrote that they landed and *"I entered one of the rooms of this house and offered several articles to the nativs in exchange for wappato [root]. they were sulkey and they positively refused to sell any. I had a small pece of port fire match in my pocket, off of which I cut a pece one inch in length & put it into the fire and took out my pocket compas and set myself down on a mat on one side of the fire, and (also showed) a magnet which was in the top of my ink stand the port fire cought and burned vehemently, which changed the colour of the fire; with the magnit I turned the needle of the compas about very briskly; which astonished and alarmed these nativs and they laid several parsles of wappato at my feet, & begged of me to take out the bad fire; to this I consented; at this moment the match being exhausted was of course extinguished and I put up the magnet &. this measure alarmed them so much that the womin and children took shelter in their beads and behind the men, all this time a very old blind man was speaking with great vehemunce, appearently imploring his god. I lit my pipe and gave them smoke, & gave the womin the full amount (value) of the roots which they had put at my feet...."*

One night was spent along the river Clark named Multnomah (Willamette River). In the morning, April 3, 1806, they proceeded to a point where the river made a bend to the east and the hills crowded in close to the west bank (within today's City of Portland), before turning around and returning to the main camp on the Columbia.

They progressed upstream, through the Great Shute above which they traded canoes for horses at every opportunity with the Indians. When they had as many animals as needed they abandoned the river and cut overland to Lewis River. They crossed the Bitterroot and the Rocky mountains. Not until reaching the Yellowstone River, a tributary of the Missouri, were they able to resume travel by water.

Three days before arriving in St. Louis, Lewis penned: *"As we moved along rapidly we saw on the banks some cows feeding, and the whole party almost involuntarily raised a shout of joy at seeing this image of civilization and domestic life.*

"Soon after we reached the little French village of La Charette, which we saluted with a discharge of four guns and three hearty cheers...."

September 23, 1806, the Lewis and Clark expedition landed in St. Louis. In two years, four months and ten days this group, dressed in buckskin and moccasins, faces brown as Indians, had traversed the continent, traveling 8,000 miles through the wilderness without losing one man.

The last entry in Lewis's journal reads: *"Tuesday, 23d, descended to the Mississippi, and round to St. Louis, where we arrived at twelve o'clock, and having fired a salute, went on shore and received the heartiest and most hospitable welcome from the whole village."*

Columbia River & Mt. Hood

The Fur Trade Era

The first attempt to colonize the mouth of the Columbia was said to have been by a group of Russians but on the sea voyage the ship was wrecked and the opportunity lost.

The second effort was by the Winship brothers of Boston. They had been involved in the trade between the North Pacific coast and China for many years but as sea otter fur became scarce they turned attention to obtaining inland furs, primarily beaver. They deemed it in their best interest to establish a permanent settlement on the Columbia. In May 1810, Nathan Winship, one of three brothers, commanded the *Albatross* over the bar and into the Columbia.

The *Albatross* sailed 45 miles upriver to where a broad fertile plain was selected as the outpost site. A log fort was constructed and a garden planted, but with the spring runoff both were dangerously close to going underwater. The fort was moved to higher ground and reassembled.

After the danger of floods lessened the colonists began having trouble with the Indians. Nathan Winship called the important chiefs to meet with him aboard the *Albatross*. They informed the captain that the Indian considered the white man a trespasser and, furthermore, a fort at the present location would interfere with their own trade with other Indians farther up the Columbia.

Captain Winship realized that without the cooperation and friendship of the Indians his settlement was doomed to fail. The outpost was abandoned and the *Albatross* sailed back over the bar. The Winship brothers were ready to make another attempt to build a colony on the Columbia when they heard of John Jacob Astor's elaborate plans. They dropped their idea and concentrated on trading in and out of the Sandwich Islands.

The Astor Expedition

John Jacob Astor was a wealthy New York fur merchant tired of battling the fur trapping and trading monopolies of Canada. The success of the Lewis and Clark expedition gave him an idea. He would become his own supplier.

Astor planned to steal the Pacific Northwest, an area rich in furs according to Lewis and Clark, by establishing a trading post at the mouth of the Columbia River and scattered outposts throughout the drainage. The rivers would be the highways for distributing supplies and trade goods and for collecting furs.

June 23, 1810, Astor was granted a charter in New York to operate the Pacific Fur Company. He kept fifty percent of the stock and divided the remaining shares among six experienced fur traders: Duncan McDougal, Alexander McKay, Donald McKenzie, David Stuart and his nephew Robert Stuart, and Wilson Price Hunt.

To assure success of the Pacific Fur Company Astor proposed to send two expeditions simultaneously — one by sea to establish the principal post and to initiate trade with the Indians, and the other overland by the route Lewis and Clark had explored. The overland expedition was to mark a number of sites for future trading posts and set trails for an overland link with New York.

Wilson Price Hunt and Donald McKenzie were to lead the overland expedition. The four other partners, with twelve clerks, nine Canadian voyageurs, an armorer and a millwright would sail aboard the *Tonquin*.

The *Tonquin* embarked from New York harbor on September 8, 1810, bound for the Horn and on to the Columbia River. Captain of the ship was Jonathan Thorn. He had distinguished himself as a naval officer but was stern, quick-tempered and ill-suited to command the fun-loving fur traders.

Captain Thorn ruled his ship with an iron hand and treated the four partners on board as if they were common seamen. He was quick to criticize, and in a letter to New York he complained the passengers *"were determined to have it said that they had been in Africa, and therefore insisted on my stopping at the Cape de Verdes. Next they said the ship must stop on the coast of Patagonia, for they must see the large and uncommon inhabitants of that place. Then they must go to the island where Robinson Crusoe had so long lived. And lastly they were determined to see the handsome inhabitants of Easter Island."*

An incident occurred at the Falkland Islands when, despite a warning by Captain Thorn, several men went ashore to hunt and failed to return promptly. The *Tonquin* set sail. Captain Thorn would have marooned them but David Stuart held a muzzle to Thorn's temple and threatened to kill him unless he gave the order to drop sail.

After rounding the Horn the *Tonquin* landed on the Sandwich Islands where, according to a letter from the Captain, the Scotch partners *"dressed in red coats, and otherwise very fantastically, and collected a number of ignorant natives around them....Then dressing in Highland plaids and kilts, and making similar arrangements, with presents of rum, wine or anything that is at hand. Then taking a number of clerks and men on shore to the very spot on which Captain Cook was killed, and each fetching off a piece of the rock or tree...."*

After disciplining a member of the crew by deserting him on one of the Sandwich Islands, Captain Thorn ordered the *Tonquin* to sail for the Columbia. They battled storm after storm on the crossing and finally arrived off the Columbia bar March 22, 1811.

The bar stretched four miles with no inviting opening in the breakers and Captain Thorn ordered his first mate, Mr. Fox, one sailor and three Canadian voyageurs to take the whaleboat and make soundings of a course for the ship to follow. According to one of the passengers, Alexander Ross, Mr. Fox protested but the captain lectured, *"If you are afraid of the water you should never have left Boston, Mr. Fox."*

Filled with misgivings, the mate climbed into the whaleboat. As it was lowered over the side he told one of Astor's partners that his uncle had been drowned in these waters a few years earlier. *"I'm going to lay me bones with the bones of me uncle,"* he said. The boat pulled toward the line of breakers and was lost from sight. Neither the boat nor any of its crew were seen again.

The *Tonquin* remained as close to shore as prudence allowed and anchored in fourteen fathoms of water. When the weather improved, Captain Thorn ordered his second mate to command a boat in another attempt to make soundings to chart a safe course for the *Tonquin*. The boat successfully located a channel but, as it returned, the river's current carried it past the *Tonquin* and out to open sea.

The *Tonquin* was helpless to send aid. The ship was perilously close to the bar. It repeatedly struck bottom and waves washed over her. It appeared imminent she would founder and be lost. Finally she drifted over the bar and into calmer water. With night descending the *Tonquin* dropped anchor in seven fathoms. On the second day at anchor two of the men from the sounding boat were found and rescued. All together eight men, within sight of their destination, had lost their lives on the treacherous Columbia bar.

Saddle Mountain

The partners of the Pacific Fur Company explored the shoreline and selected a spot on the south bank ten miles inland for their trading post. The site was sheltered by a wooded hill on the south and southwest, accessible from the sea and easily reached by canoes from upriver. They named this place Fort Astoria.

Alexander Ross, one of the clerks, described the scene: "*From the site of the establishment the eye could wander over a varied and interesting scene. The extensive sound, with its rocky shores, lay in front; the breakers on the bar, rolling in wild confusion, closed the view to the west; on the east, the country as far as the Sound had a wild and varied aspect; while towards the south, the impervious and magnificent forest darkened the landscape as far as the eye could reach. The place thus selected for the emporium of the West might challenge the whole continent to produce a spot of equal extent presenting more difficulties to the settler: studded with gigantic trees of almost incredible size, many of them measuring fifty feet in girth, and so close together, and intermingled with huge rocks, as to make it work of no ordinary labor to level and clear the ground. With this task before us every man, from the highest to the lowest, was armed with an axe in one hand and a gun in the other: the former for attacking the woods, the latter for defense against the savage hordes which were constantly prowling about. . . .*

"*. . . Many of the party had never handled an axe before and but few of them knew how to use a gun, but necessity, the mother of invention, soon taught us both. After placing our guns in some secure place at hand, and viewing the height and the breadth of the tree to be cut down, the party, with some labor, would erect a scaffold round it; this done, four men — for that was the number appointed to each of those huge trees — would then mount the scaffold, and commence cutting at the height of eight or ten feet from the ground, the handles of our axes varying, according to circumstances, from two and a half to five feet in length. At every other stroke a look was cast round to see that all was safe; but the least rustling among the bushes caused a general stop. More or less time was thus lost in anxious suspense. After listening and looking round, the party resumed their labor, cutting and looking about alternately. In this manner the day would be spent and often to little purpose, as night often set in before the tree begun with in the morning was half cut down. Indeed, it sometimes required two days or more to fell one tree; but when nearly cut through, it would be viewed fifty different times, and from as many different positions, to ascertain where it was likely to fall and to warn parties of the danger.*

"*There is an art in felling a tree as well as in planting one, but unfortunately none of us had learned that art, and hours together would be spent in conjectures and discussions; one calling out that it would fall here; another, there. In short, there were as many opinions as there were individuals about it; and at last, when all hands were assembled to witness the fall, how often were we disappointed! The tree would still stand erect, bidding defiance to our efforts, while every now and then some of the most impatient or foolhardy would venture to jump on the scaffold and give a blow or two more. Much time was often spent in this desultory manner before the mighty tree gave way, but it seldom came to the ground. So thick was the forest, and so close the trees together, that in its fall it would often rest its ponderous top on some other friendly tree. Sometimes a number of them would hang together, keeping us in awful suspense, and giving us double labor to extricate the one from the other, and when we had so far succeeded, the removal of the monster stump was the work of days. The tearing up of the roots was equally arduous, although less dangerous; and when this last operation was got through, both tree and stump had to be blown to pieces by gunpowder before either could be removed from the spot.*

"*Nearly two months of this laborious and incessant toil had passed, and we had scarcely yet an acre of ground cleared. In the meantime three of our men were killed by natives, two more wounded by the falling of trees, and one had his hand blown off by gunpowder.*"

The first of June Captain Thorn announced he was going on a trading cruise along the coast, as Mr. Astor had authorized him. He left the men on shore almost defenseless against the ever-increasing number of Indians who came to view the felling of trees and construction of log buildings and stockade. The *Tonquin* carried with her the majority of the fort's supplies and trade goods.

On June 5 the *Tonquin* crossed the bar. The captain and crew were accompanied by one of the partners, Alexander McKay, and an Indian guide named Lamazee. They turned the ship north and ranged along the coast.

The *Tonquin* missed by some months the time of her expected return to Fort Astoria. Indians told vague and conflicting rumors about the fate of the ship and it engendered fear in the men. By all accounts the *Tonquin* had been destroyed.

October 12 three Chinook Indians were fitted out and sent off, and told not to return until they had proof resolving the mystery of the missing ship. The three had not progressed far before meeting an Indian on his way to the fort with news of the *Tonquin's* tragic end. The Chinooks turned around and accompanied the Indian to Fort Astoria where it is told that he reported: "*My name is Kasiascall, but the Chinooks and other Indians hereabout call me Lamazee. I belong to the Wickanook tribe of Indians near Nootka Sound. I have often been on board ships. The whites call me Jack. I understand most of the languages that are spoken along the coast. I can speak some Chinook, too. I have been twice at this place before, once by land and once by sea. I saw the ship Tonquin; Captain Thorn was her commander. I went on board of her at Woody Point Harbor in June last. We remained there for two days. We then sailed for Vancouver's Island, and just as we got to it a gale of wind drove us to sea, and it was three days before we got back again. The fourth morning we cast anchor in Eyuck Whoola, Newcetu Bay. There we remained for some days, Indians going and coming, but not much trade. One day the Indians came on board in great numbers, but did not trade much although they had plenty of skins. The prices offered did not please the Indians, so they carried back their furs again. The day following the chiefs came on board, and as usual asked the Captain to show them such and such things, and state the lowest price, which he accordingly did. They did not, however, trade, but pressed the Captain for presents, which he refused. The chiefs left the ship displeased at what they called the stingy conduct in the Captain, as they were accustomed to receive trifling presents from the traders on the coast.*

"*In the evening of the same day, Mr. McKay and myself went on shore and were well received by the chiefs, and saw a great many sea-otter skins with the Indians. We both returned to the ship the same evening. Next day the Indians came off to trade in great numbers. On their coming alongside, the Captain ordered the boarding-netting to be put up round the ship, and would not allow more than ten on board at a time; but just as the trade had commenced, an Indian was detected cutting the boarding-netting with a knife in order to get on board. On being detected he instantly jumped into one of the canoes which were alongside and made his escape. The Captain then, turning round, bade the chiefs to call him back. The chiefs smiled and said nothing, which irritated the Captain, and he immediately laid hold of two of the chiefs and threatened to hang them up unless they caused the delinquent to be brought back to be punished. The moment the chiefs were seized, all the Indians fled from the ship in consternation. The chiefs were kept on board all night with a guard over them. Food was offered them, but they would neither eat nor drink. Next day, however, the offender was brought to the ship and delivered up, when the Captain ordered him to be stripped and tied up, but did not flog him. He was then dismissed. The chiefs were also liberated and left the ship, refusing with distain a present that was offered them, and vowing vengeance on the whites for the insult received.*

"...the Indians began to flock about the ship, both men and women, in great crowds, with their furs; and certainly I myself thought that there was not the least danger, particularly as the women accompanied the men to trade; but I was surprised that the Captain did not put the netting up. It was the first time I ever saw a ship trade there without adopting that precaution. As soon as the Indians arrived, the Captain, relying no doubt on the apparent reconciliation which had taken place between McKay and the chiefs on shore, and wishing, perhaps, to atone for the insult he had offered the latter, flew from one extreme to the other, receiving them with open arms and admitting them on board without reserve and without the usual precautions. The trade went on briskly, and at the Captain's own price, the Indians throwing the goods received into the canoes, which were alongside with the women in them; but in doing so they managed to conceal their knives about their persons, which circumstance was noticed by one of the men aloft, then by myself, and we warned the Captain of it; but he treated the suggestions, as usual, with a smile of contempt and no more was said about it; but in a moment or two afterwards the Captain began to suspect something himself and was in the act of calling Mr. McKay to him when the Indians in an instant raised the hideous yell of death, which echoed from stem to stern of the devoted ship. The women in the canoes immediately pushed off, and the massacre began. The conflict was bloody but short. The savages, with their naked knives and horrid yells, rushed on the unsuspecting and defenseless whites, who were dispersed all over the ship, and in five minutes' time the vessel was their own. McKay was the first man who fell. He shot one Indian, but was instantly killed and thrown overboard, and so sudden was the surprise that the Captain had scarcely time to draw from his pocket a clasp-knife, with which he defended himself desperately, killed two, and wounded several more, till at last he fell dead in the crowd. The last man I saw alive was Stephen Weeks, the armorer. In the midst of the carnage, I leaped overboard, as did several other Indians, and we were taken up by the women in the canoes, who were yelling, whooping, and crying like so many fiends about the ship; but before I had got two gunshots from the ship, and not ten minutes after I had left her, she blew up in the air with a fearful explosion, filling the whole place with broken fragments and mutilated bodies. The sight was terrific and overwhelming. Weeks must have been the man who blew up the ship, and by that awful act of revenge 175 Indians perished, and some of the canoes, although at a great distance off, had a narrow escape. The melancholy and fatal catastrophe spread desolation, lamentation, and terror through the whole tribe.

"...I had started long ago with the tidings of her [the Tonquin] tragical end, but falling sick, I was prevented from coming sooner...."

At first Lamazee's story was believed but in the days ahead other Indians came forward to tell their version, particularly regarding Lamazee's part in the treachery. They claimed that early in the morning of the *Tonquin's* fatal day Lamazee had induced the Captain to send a boat to shore. Six men were in the boat in addition to Lamazee. When the ship blew up the six tried to escape and it was Lamazee who headed a party that captured the unfortunate men. They were brought to camp and *"first tortured with savage cruelty, and then all massacred in the most inhumane manner"*.

The destruction of the *Tonquin* left Fort Astoria nearly defenseless, without adequate supplies and trade items. The men were left without hope except for the anticipation of the overland expedition working its way west.

Duncan McDougal, commander of Fort Astoria, sent word to all the important Indian chiefs in the neighborhood calling them to a meeting. He told the Indians they should not cause the white man harm, that the white man always revenged bad deeds. He pointed out the *Tonquin* had been blown up and many more Indians than whites had perished.

He held a small vial in front of him so the Indians could see it clearly. His fingers gingerly toyed with the cork. *"I only have to remove the cork. If you show any sign of hostility against us I will let the disease loose among you — the smallpox,"* he threatened. The Indians shrank back in fear. They pleaded with McDougal not to uncork the vial.

Fort Astoria (Ft. George)

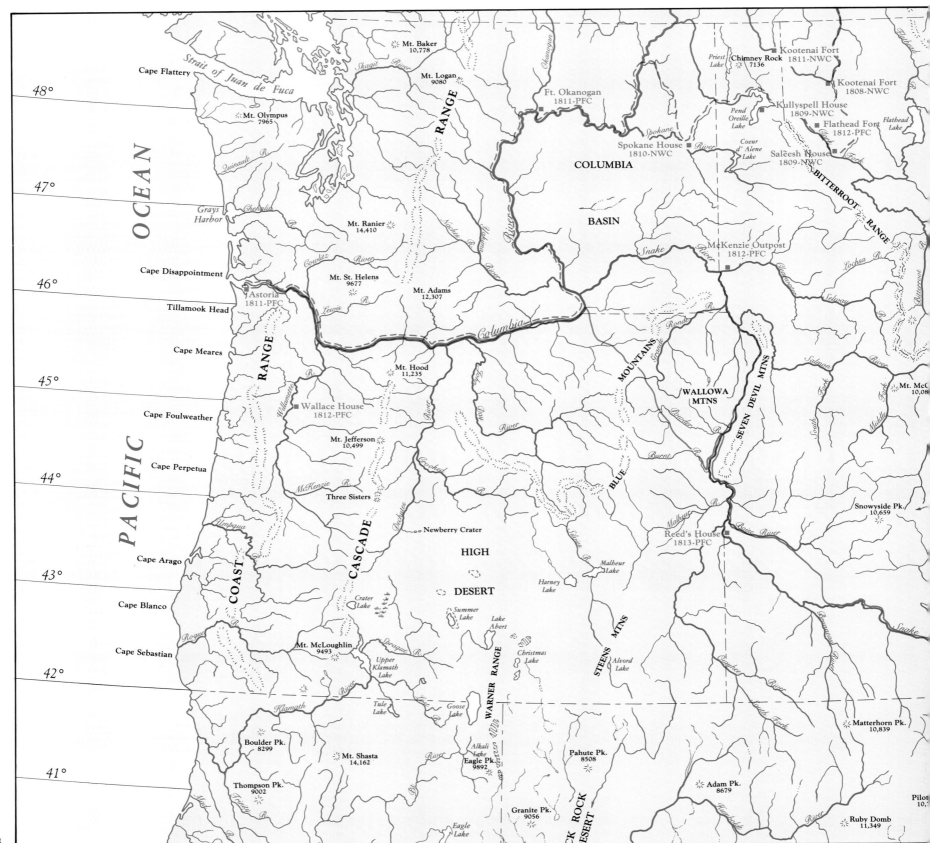

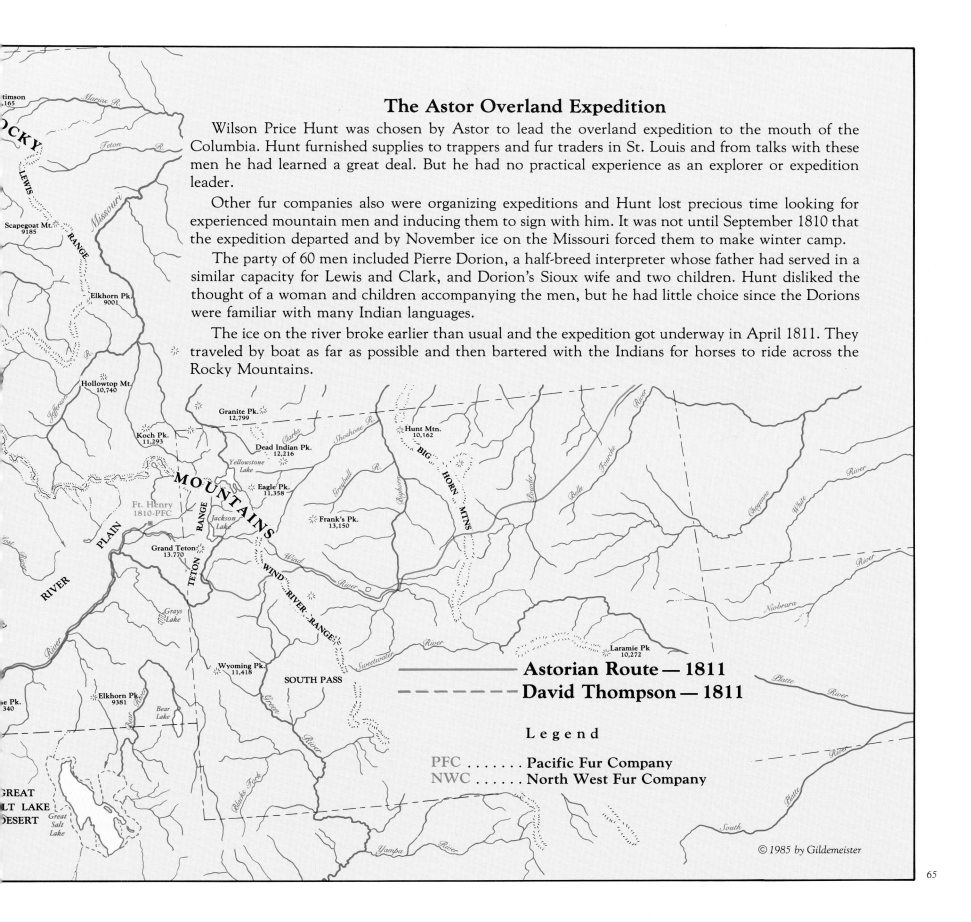

The Astor Overland Expedition

Wilson Price Hunt was chosen by Astor to lead the overland expedition to the mouth of the Columbia. Hunt furnished supplies to trappers and fur traders in St. Louis and from talks with these men he had learned a great deal. But he had no practical experience as an explorer or expedition leader.

Other fur companies also were organizing expeditions and Hunt lost precious time looking for experienced mountain men and inducing them to sign with him. It was not until September 1810 that the expedition departed and by November ice on the Missouri forced them to make winter camp.

The party of 60 men included Pierre Dorion, a half-breed interpreter whose father had served in a similar capacity for Lewis and Clark, and Dorion's Sioux wife and two children. Hunt disliked the thought of a woman and children accompanying the men, but he had little choice since the Dorions were familiar with many Indian languages.

The ice on the river broke earlier than usual and the expedition got underway in April 1811. They traveled by boat as far as possible and then bartered with the Indians for horses to ride across the Rocky Mountains.

Astorian Route — 1811

David Thompson — 1811

Legend

PFC . . . . **Pacific Fur Company**
NWC . . . . . . **North West Fur Company**

© 1985 by Gildemeister

That fall they reached a tributary of the Snake River, turned their 180 horses loose and switched to fifteen canoes. They expected an easy voyage downstream to Fort Astoria. The first day they made 30 miles but in time they cursed the fact they ever took to the water. They reached the Snake and found rapids and great falls that cascaded over solid basalt flows.

Astor's overland expedition found itself in the most dire situation. Without horses each man was forced to shoulder a heavy pack, they had no maps or information about the general lay of the country, winter was fast approaching, and they had only five days of food on hand.

Hunt divided the party into four groups and they fanned out hoping that would increase their odds of coming across game, though they rarely did.

Two groups followed the Snake. On one side Hunt led eighteen men and the same number were led on the other side by Ramsay Crooks. Crooks, a native of Scotland, had served in the North West Company and was well experienced in the ways of the mountain man and living off the land.

The two groups lost contact with each other until the morning of December 6 when Crooks and his companions were heard across the swash of the river pleading desperately for food. Hunt's party had come across and killed a horse the night before and a crude canoe was made Indian-fashion by stretching horsehide over a frame of willows. Meat was ferried to the men and Crooks returned to confer with Hunt.

During the night the boat was washed away. In the morning Crooks joined Hunt's party but in his weakened condition he could not keep up. Hunt faced a painful decision — to stay with the slowest and risk certain and terrible death for all or to push ahead through the mountains before the full fury of winter hit. In the end Ramsay Crooks and John Day, the men in the worst condition, were left with a band of Snake Indians.

The main party trudged on. The men broke into smaller groups and straggled across the desolate sagebrush plain scarred by the winding Snake River. They existed on occasional game, and some of the men resorted to chewing on their moccasins for lack of anything else.

Where the Snake River squeezed through the mountains in a deep gorge most of the party reunited. On the day before Christmas this group cut away from the river and started through the mountains. In all there were 32 white men, three Indians, the pregnant squaw and two children of Pierre Dorion, and five starving horses. Stumbling up draws and over windblown ridges, battling cold and drifting snow, they made their weary way at the rate of fourteen miles a day. At last they topped out overlooking the broad Powder river valley cradled by lofty mountain peaks. They skirted the valley and climbed through bleak, sagebrush hills.

It was in this desolate country, on the next to the last day of 1811, that Pierre Dorion's wife went into labor. Dorion announced he was staying with his wife and their children. He told the others the family would catch up after the baby was born.

Hunt's party continued. Within a few miles one of the men gave up, saying he could walk no farther. Hunt put the man on the strongest horse and added his pack to his own. Each step was torture. Each mile only added more distance to this death march.

They broke over a hill and unexpectedly found a hidden, oval-shaped valley (Grande Ronde Valley) surrounded by snowy mountains. The valley floor was free of snow. And there, far below beside a meandering stream, were Indian lodges, grazing horses and a number of dogs that had spotted strangers high on the ridge and begun to bark.

Hunt was able to trade the Indians a few trinkets for four horses, three dogs and some roots. A more hopeful camp was set that evening and in the morning Pierre Dorion and his family came in, his wife holding a new-born infant wrapped in a blanket in her arms.

Elkhorn Range of the Blue Mountains

It was the first day of the new year, 1812. The men decided to lay over and make an occasion of it in defiance of their hardships and the fact that the New Year's banquet was dog meat and horse flesh.

The following morning Hunt led the ragged group into the Blue Mountains. The snow was waist deep and they took turns breaking trail. The sun hid behind a thick layer of storm clouds. It was foggy and cold. On January 6 they crossed the divide and started down. The snow depth decreased and the temperature warmed. On this day the Dorion baby died and was buried beside the trail.

A shout rose from those leading the march when they dropped below tree line. An Indian village could be clearly seen. They pushed forward, Hunt in the lead, and when they reached the village they found the Indians very prosperous. The tribe lived in 34 lodges constructed of mats laid over wood frames, they were dressed in buckskin shirts and leggings with robes of buffalo and deer skin. Hunt entered one of the lodges to barter for horses and dogs and was surprised to find the Indians in possession of brass kettles, axes and other articles of civilization. It showed they were in direct trade with the sea coast. Hunt inquired if there was a great river in the vicinity and was relieved to learn there was, and only a two-day march away.

For several days they stayed in the village, feasting on animals purchased from the Indians, allowing the stragglers to catch up. The reassembled expedition traveled to the Columbia River and followed it downstream to the gorge. At the bottom of the last series of falls Hunt purchased canoes from the Indians and the party took to the water.

February 15 the remnants of Astor's overland expedition were swept around a cape and came within sight of Fort Astoria. Paddles were taken up, blades dug into the water and with much hurrahing from those in the canoes and shouts of encouragement from shore, they turned out of the current. Moments later the men, tears staining their cheeks, were hugging each other and dancing for the sheer joy of it.

Included in the greeters were Donald McKenzie and a small party who had split from the group on Snake River. They had stayed on the east side of the river as it turned north and climbed into the Seven Devils Mountains. They wandered and suffered 21 days before dropping back to the Snake and following it to the Columbia where they acquired canoes and floated to Fort Astoria.

A celebration began with the hoisting of the Stars and Stripes and firing a salute. The men sang and danced and feasted on fish, beaver and venison in addition to a hefty allowance of grog. Late that night the mood turned serious as the various members told of the misfortune and tragedy they had faced. And at the end, concern was expressed for the men still out on the trail: Ramsay Crooks, John Day and three Canadians.

They need not have worried about the Canadians who had walked to a Shoshone village where they spent the winter well cared for. But Crooks and Day were facing starvation and death as the others celebrated. It was three months later that Crooks and Day were discovered and Crooks was able to relate:

"After being left by Mr. Hunt, we remained for some time with the Snakes [Indians], *who were very kind to us. When they had anything to eat we ate also; but they soon departed, and being themselves without*

provisions, of course they left us without any. We had to provide for ourselves the best way we could. As soon, therefore, as the Indians went off, we collected some brushwood and coarse hay and made a sort of booth, or wigwam, to shelter us from the cold. We then collected some firewood; but before we got things in order, John Day grew so weak that when he sat down he could not rise again without help. Following the example of the Indians I dug up roots for our sustenance, but not knowing how to cook them, we were nearly poisoned. In this plight we unfortunately let the fire go out, and for a day and night we both lay in a torpid state, unable to strike fire, or to collect dry fuel. We had now been a day without food, or even water to drink, and death appeared inevitable. But Providence is ever kind. Two straggling Indians, happening to come our way, relieved us. They made us a fire, got us some water, and gave us something to eat; but seeing some roots we had collected for food lying in a corner, they gave us to understand that they would poison us if we ate them. If we had had a fire, those very roots would have been our first food, for we had nothing else to eat; and we can tell but the hand of a kind and superintending Providence was in all this? These poor fellows stayed with us the greater part of two days and gave us at their departure about two pounds of venison. We were really sorry to lose them.

"On the same day, after the Indians had left us, a very large wolf came prowling about our hut, when John Day, with great exertion and good luck, shot the ferocious animal dead, and to this fortunate hit I think we owed our lives. The flesh of the wolf we cut up and dried and laid it by for some future emergency, and in the meantime feasted upon the skin; nor did we throw away the bones, but pounded them between stones, and with some roots made a kind of broth, which in our present circumstances we found very good. After we had recovered our strength a little and were able to walk, we betook ourselves to the mountains in search of game; and when unsuccessful in the chase we had recourse to our dried wolf. For two months we wandered about, barely sustaining life with our utmost exertions. All this time we kept traveling to and fro, until we happened, by mere chance, to fall on the Umatallow River [Umatilla River]; and then, following it, we made the Columbia on the fifteenth day of April according to our reckoning. Our clothes being all torn and worn out, we suffered severely from cold; but on reaching this place, the Indians were very kind to us. One man, an old gray-headed Indian called Yeckatapam, in particular treated us like a father. After resting ourselves for two days with the good old man and his people, we set off, following the current in the delusive hope of being able to reach our friends at the mouth of the Columbia, as the Indians gave us to understand that white men had gone down there in the winter, which we supposed must have been Mr. Hunt and his party.

"We had proceeded on our journey nine days without interruption and were not far from the Falls, which the Indians made us comprehend by uttering the work 'tumm', which we understood to mean noise or fall, when one morning as we were sitting near the river, gazing on the beautiful stream before us, the Indians in considerable numbers collected round us in the usual friendly manner. After some little time, however, one of them got up and under pretense of measuring the length of my rifle with his bow, took it in his hands; another in the same manner, and at the same moment, took John Day's rifle from him. The moment our guns were in their possession the two Indians darted out of the crowd to some distance, and assuming a menacing attitude, pointed them at us; in the same instant all the others fled from us and joined the two who had carried off our guns. All began to intimate to us by signs, in the most uproarious and wild manner, that some of their people had been killed by the whites, and threatened to kill us in turn. In this critical conjunction John Day drew his knife with the intention of rushing upon the fellows to get hold of his gun; but I pointed out to him the folly of such a step, which must have instantly proved fatal to us, and he desisted.

"The Indians then closed in upon us, with guns pointed and bows drawn, on all sides, and by force stripped us of our clothes, ammunition, knives, and everything else, leaving us naked as the day we were born, and by their movements and gestures it appeared evident that there was a disposition on their part to kill us; but, after a long and angry debate, in which two or three old men seemed to befriend us, they made signs for us to be off. Seeing the savages determined, and more of them still collecting, we slowly turned round and went up the river again, expecting every moment to receive a ball or an arrow. After traveling some little distance we looked back and saw the savages quarreling about the division of the booty; but fearing pursuit, we left the river and took to the hills. All that day we traveled without tasting food, and at night concealed ourselves among the rocks, without fire, food, or clothing. Next day we drew near to the river and picked up some fishbones at a deserted Indian encampment. With these we returned to the rocks again, and pounded them with stones, tried to eat a little, but could not manage to swallow any. That night, also, we hid ourselves among the rocks, but at last we resolved to keep by the river, and as it seemed impossible to avoid death, either by the Indians or starvation, to brave all dangers in the attempt to reach our good old friend Yeckatapam, and Providence still guarded us.

"Soon after we arrived at the river we unexpectedly fell on a small Indian hut, with only two old people and a child in it. We approached with hesitating and doubtful steps, but on entering the solitary wigwam, the poor inmates were more frightened than ourselves; and had they had timely notice of our approach, they would have certainly fled. The good people, however, gave us fish, broth, and roots to eat, and this was the first food we had tasted, and the first fire we had seen, for four days and four nights. Our feet were severely cut and bleeding for want of shoes, yet we lost no time, but set off, and arrived here with our good old friend Yeckatapam. He received us again with open arms and gave us these skins to cover our nakedness as ye now see.

"The good old man then killed a horse, which his people cut up and dried for us, and with that supply we had resolved to set out this very day and retrace our steps back again to St. Louis overland, and when you came in sight we were just in the act of tying up our little bundles, regretting, most of all, that we had no means of recompensing our good and faithful friend Yeckatapam."

A group of fur traders, led by Robert Stuart, was canoeing down the Columbia bound for Fort Astoria with 2,500 beaver pelts from the Okanogan country. Early one morning, near the mouth of Umatilla River, they noticed a large congregation of Indians and were hailed in English to "Come on shore". Stuart commanded the four canoes be steered to the Indian side and there found two men so emaciated that for a moment they were not recognized as Ramsay Crooks and John Day.

The Indians were rewarded for their kindness; Yeckatapam received a new set of clothes and the Americans departed downriver. They reached Astoria on May 12 to a hearty welcome and the good news that the company ship *Beaver* had arrived from New York with a full load of supplies and a reinforcement of men.

The Pacific Fur Company

Greeting the visitor to Fort Astoria was an American flag flying from a tall spar pole. Four cannons afforded a commanding position of the river and stockade walls, built of logs set vertically with the sharp-pointed ends fifteen feet off the ground, protected sleeping quarters, a dining hall, warehouses, a blacksmith's forge and carpenter's workshop. A gallery ran around the inside of the stockade and holes had been cut so muskets could be fired through them. Two guard houses, on opposite corners, protected access with a pair of six-pounders. A steady watch was kept.

Fort Astoria was the meeting place, in May 1812, of the active members of the Pacific Fur Company, minus John Jacob Astor. They met to plan the campaign to occupy the territory and resolved that each partner would head an expedition to establish a series of six far-flung trading posts throughout the Columbia drainage: Fort Okanogan (near the junction of the Okanogan and Columbia rivers), Fort Spokane (near Spokane, Washington), Fort Kootenai (near Jennings, Montana), Flathead Post (near Heron, Montana), She Whaps Post (near Kamloops, British Columbia), Wallace House (near Salem, Oregon), and a temporary post on Henry's Fork of the Snake River (between Elgin and St. Anthony, Idaho).

The trappers and traders scattered across the vast wilderness while Robert Stuart and a small party started overland on horseback with dispatches and company records bound for St. Louis and ultimately New York. They followed the Columbia to the land of the Wallah-Wallah Indians, then crossed the mountains to the high desert bordering the Snake River without incident. But beyond the headwaters of the Snake a war party of Crow Indians swept down on camp and drove off the horses.

The white men were left afoot. Anything they could not carry was burned. Stuart decided against crossing deeper into Crow lands even though it would bring them to the buffalo country most quickly. He chose a longer northern route that carried its own danger of starvation. They wandered about for five days and nights with nothing to eat. On the sixth day one of the Canadians, gaunt and wild from hunger, approached Stuart, saying, *"It is better one should die than that all should perish."* He proposed they draw lots to see which of them should be sacrificed.

Stuart reprimanded the man severely. Under no circumstances would a party under his command resort to cannibalism. He ordered the others to take away the man's gun. The following day they came across a solitary buffalo bull which they managed to kill.

On November 2 they built a log house for winter camp. Buffalo roamed the area and the men thought they would be able to pass the time tolerably but an Indian war party discovered them. They had to move. The Indians did not find them again and on March 20 they broke camp and set off in two canoes built during the winter. By mid-April they reached the Missouri and were in St. Louis by the end of the month. They were the first to take the route of what was later to become the Oregon Trail.

The Selling of Astoria

The British North West Company developed an early interest in the Pacific Northwest. At the time of the Astor expedition the company already had located four trading posts in the Columbia drainage at Kootenai House, Kullyspell House, Saleesh House, Spokane House and outposts on lakes Coeur d'Alene and Pend d'Oreille.

One of the most enterprising employees of the North West Company was David Thompson who had spent thirteen years with the Hudson's Bay Company before switching allegiance in 1797. He was responsible for establishing most of the trading posts on the Columbia and its tributaries. When Thompson heard of Astor's plans with the Pacific Fur Company he made a mad dash for the mouth of the Columbia, only to arrive July 15, 1811, and find the American Fort Astoria under construction.

Alexander Ross, a clerk with the Astor expedition, said of Thompson's visit: *"On the fifteenth of July we were rather surprised at the unexpected arrival of a North-West proprietor at Astoria, and still more so at the free and cordial reception given to an opponent. Mr. Thompson, North-West like, came dashing down the Columbia in a light canoe, manned with eight Iroquois and an interpreter, chiefly men from the vicinity of Montreal. McDougall [in command of Astoria] received him like a brother....His visit had evidently no other object but to discourage us, a maneuver of the North-West policy to extend their own trade at the expense of ours, but he failed. The dangers and difficulties, which he took great pains to paint in their worst colors, did not deter us...."*

After his short and unsuccessful visit at Astoria Thompson returned upriver. The Astorians went about opening up the country to their fur trade. The North Westerners stayed mostly to the north until the fall of 1813 when, under the command of John George McTavish, a squadron of ten canoes carrying 75 North Westerners swooped down on Astoria with the news that England and America were at war. All Atlantic ports were blockaded and warships were on their way, and expected any day, to take possession of Astoria.

McTavish set his camp within yards of the fort. They would wait for the warships and then take possession, but while they waited they found themselves in an embarrassing situation. They were without food. Days stretched one into another.

Gabriel Franchere, a clerk at the fort, reported that the North Westerners became *"weary at length with applying to us incessantly for food (which we furnished with a sparing hand), unable either to retrace their steps through the wilderness or to remain in their present position, they came to the conclusion of proposing to buy of us the whole establishment."*

The two commanders, McDougal for the Astorians and McTavish for the North Westerners, entered into negotiations. The Americans wanted to conclude the sale of their holdings as quickly as possible, before the British warships entered the river and claimed them as a prize. McTavish was in no hurry. He tried to drag out the discussions, hoping the North West Company could take possession without having to complete a purchase.

Alexander Ross described how the sale was finally consummated: *"One morning before daylight Messrs. McDougall and McKenzie summoned all hands together, seventy-two in number, and after a brief statement of the views of the North West in reference to the negotiation, ordered the bastions to be manned, the guns to be loaded and pointed, and matches lighted. In an instant every man was at his post, and the gates shut. At eight o'clock a message was sent to McTavish, giving him two hours, and no more, either to sign the bills or break off negotiations altogether and remove to some other quarters. By eleven o'clock the bills were finally and formally signed, and Astoria was delivered up to the North West Company...."*

The date of the signing was October 23, 1813. Fort Astoria, all furs, supplies, trade goods and all the Oregon country and outposts controlled by the Pacific Fur Company were sold for $40,000. A week later the British warship, the sloop *Raccoon* with 26 guns and under the command of Captain William Black, entered the river. The Captain was disappointed to learn of the sale and transfer of Fort Astoria. He had hoped to capture the fort. His comment on first viewing the settlement was: *"What is this, the fort I have heard so much of? Great God, I could batter it down with a four-pounder in two hours!"*

Captain Black took official control of the Oregon country. He lowered the Stars and Stripes and ran up the Union Jack to flutter in the ocean breeze. He renamed the outpost Fort George. The light of American occupation was extinguished.

The North West and Hudson's Bay Companies

The North West Company held control of the Pacific Northwest, but in the interior and to the north a fight for supremacy was waged with the older and more established Hudson's Bay Company. Rival outposts were burned, trappers murdered and furs stolen. To gain an edge in trade, alcohol was introduced as a commerce item. In one two-year period, nearly 200,000 gallons of liquor were expended to the Indians by the rivals.

By 1820 the war between the two giant companies was taking a financial toll. Officials met in London and after lengthy negotiations a truce was made. The companies merged under the name of the older company, the Hudson's Bay Company.

George Simpson was appointed governor of all Company territory west of the Rocky Mountains. To familiarize himself with the country under his command he made a canoe trip west. On the Athabasca River he overtook another Company party which included the man appointed Chief Factor on the Columbia District. September 26, 1824, Simpson wrote of his initial impressions of Dr. John McLoughlin, a name destined to become familiar to the Northwest: "[He] *was such a figure as I should not like to meet in a dark Night in one of the bye lanes in the neighborhood of London, dressed in Clothes that had once been fashionable, but now covered with a thousand patches of different Colors, his beard would do honor to the chin of a Grizzly Bear....*"

Frozen Beaver Pond

Simpson and McLoughlin arrived together at Fort George in early November and immediately began revamping the Columbia District. They agreed the headquarters near the ocean was poorly situated, not conveniently reached from the interior posts nor by the regular routes of the Indians. They searched for a new site surrounded by plenty of farmland and chose a spot on the north bank 75 miles from the mouth of the Columbia River. It was relatively level land that could be easily farmed, sheltered from the ocean winds but still accessible by ship. The view was grand. A line of lofty, snow-capped peaks dominated the eastern horizon and to the south lay the broad expanse of the Willamette Valley.

Land was cleared and a fort constructed from logs. Simpson, before returning to the east, dedicated Fort Vancouver on March 19, 1825. Four years later the buildings were torn down and moved nearer the river. The rebuilt stockade and buildings formed a parallelogram around seven acres, the log stockade was 20 feet high and the gate protected by a brass cannon. Inside were a residence for the chief factor, dormitory for the employees, dining hall, shops and storehouses.

The fertile ground surrounding the fort was planted in potatoes, peas, wheat, oats, barley and Indian corn. Twenty-seven cattle were brought in and turned out in the pasture. In order to build the herd Dr. McLoughlin gave orders that no cattle were to be killed for the use of the fort except one bull calf annually. The tables were supplied with fresh and salted fish, venison and wild fowl.

Fort Vancouver was the trade center of an area from the coast near San Francisco Bay on the south to the Russian settlements on the north and inland to the Rocky Mountains. Posts were established like spokes from the hub of a wheel and supplied by brigades of canoe voyageurs who returned downriver with furs.

Rather than relying entirely on trade with the Indians as its source of fur the Company, in 1824, sent out the first of many great trapping expeditions. Large groups of company trappers and free trappers, their Indian wives and half-breed children moved slowly through the countryside. They scoured every stream and creek, driving the beaver to the brink of extinction.

Ft. Vancouver

Introduction to a Trapper

The outfit of a trapper is generally a rifle, a pound of powder, and four pounds of lead, with a bullet mould, seven traps, an axe, a hatchet, a knife and awl, a camp kettle, two blankets, and, where supplies are plenty, seven pounds of flour. He has, generally, two or three horses, to carry himself and his baggage and peltries. Two trappers commonly go together, for the purpose of mutual assistance and support — a larger party could not escape the eyes of the Indians. It is a service of peril; and even more so at present than formerly, since they have got into the habit of trafficking peltries with the traders, have learnt the value of the beaver, and look upon the trappers as poachers, who are filching the riches from their streams and interfering with their market. They make no hesitation, therefore, to murder the solitary trapper, and thus destroy a competitor, while they possess themselves of his spoils. It is with regret we add, too, that this hostility has in many cases been instigated by traders, desirous of injuring their rivals, but who have themselves often reaped the fruits of the mischief they have sown.

When two trappers undertake any considerable stream, their mode of proceeding is to hide their horses in some lonely glen where they can graze unobserved. They then build a small hut, dig out a canoe from a cotton-wood tree, and in this poke along shore silently in the evening, and set their traps. These they revisit in the same silent way at daybreak. When they take any beaver, they bring it home, skin it, stretch the skin on sticks to dry, and feast upon the flesh. The body, hung up before the fire, turns by its own weight, and is roasted in a superior style. The tail is the trapper's titbit; it is cut off, put on the end of a stick, and toasted, and is considered even a greater dainty than the tongue or the marrow-bone of a buffalo.

With all their silence and caution, however, the poor trappers cannot always escape their hawk-eyed enemies. Their trail has been discovered, perhaps, and followed up for many a mile; or their smoke has been seen curling up out of the secret glen, or has been scented by the savages, whose sense of smell is almost as acute as that of sight. Sometimes they are pounced upon when in the act of setting their traps; at other times, they are roused from their sleep by the horrid war-whoop; or, perhaps, have a bullet or an arrow whistling about their ears, in the midst of one of their beaver banquets. In this way they are picked off, from time to time, and nothing is known of them, until, perchance, their bones are found bleaching in some lonely ravine, or on the banks of some nameless stream, which from that time is called after them. Many of the small streams beyond the mountains thus perpetuate the names of unfortunate trappers that have been murdered on their banks.

Adventures of Captain Bonneville
by Washington Irving

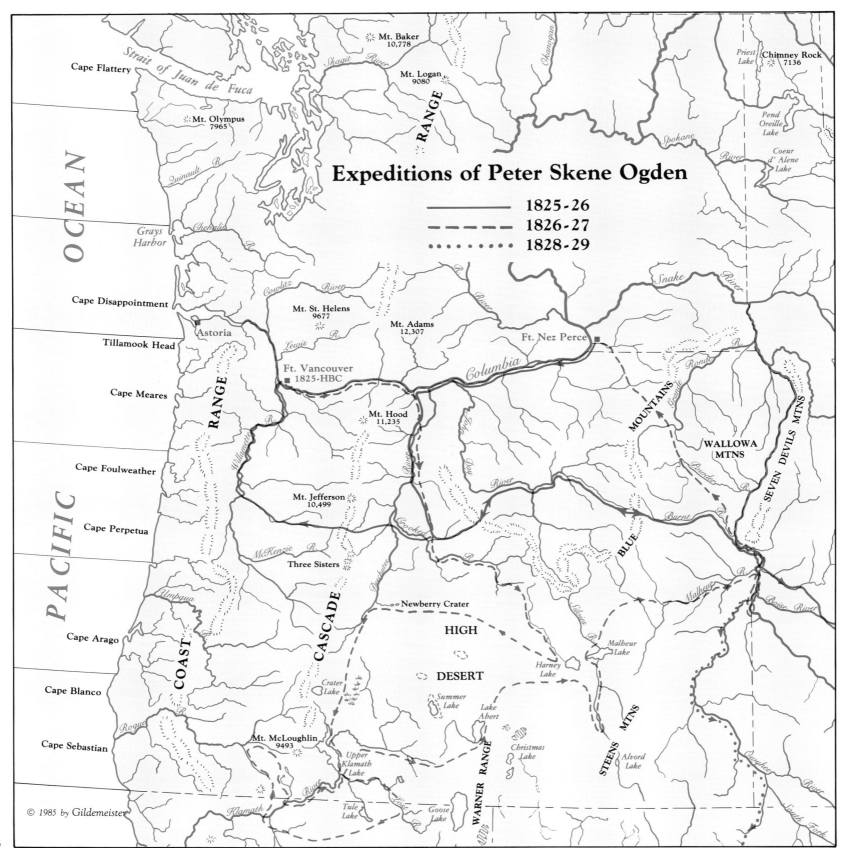

Expeditions of Peter Skene Ogden

————————	1825-26
– – – – – – –	1826-27
··········	1828-29

OCEAN

PACIFIC

Cape Flattery

Strait of Juan de Fuca

Mt. Baker
10,778

Mt. Logan
9080

RANGE

Priest Lake

Chimney Rock
7136

Mt. Olympus
7965

Quinault R.

Skagit River

Okanogan

Pend Oreille Lake

Spokane

River

Coeur d'Alene Lake

Grays Harbor

Chehalis

Cowlitz River

Mt. St. Helens
9677

Mt. Adams
12,307

Snake River

Cape Disappointment

Astoria

Lewis R.

Ft. Nez Perce

Tillamook Head

RANGE

Ft. Vancouver
1825-HBC

Columbia

MOUNTAINS

Ronde

R.

Cape Meares

R.

Mt. Hood
11,235

River

Grande Ronde

WALLOWA MTNS

SEVEN DEVILS MTNS

Cape Foulweather

Willamette

River

River

Burnt

R.

Cape Perpetua

Mt. Jefferson
10,499

McKenzie R.

Crooked

River

BLUE

COAST

Three Sisters

Deschutes R.

R.

Malheur

Boise River

Cape Arago

CASCADE

Newberry Crater

HIGH

Silvies R.

Malheur Lake

Cape Blanco

Crater Lake

DESERT

Harney Lake

STEENS MTNS

Umpqua

Mt. McLoughlin
9493

Summer Lake

Lake Abert

Christmas Lake

Alvord Lake

Cape Sebastian

Rogue R.

Upper Klamath Lake

WARNER RANGE

South Fork

Klamath River

Tule Lake

Lost R.

Goose Lake

Owyhee River

PACIFIC

© 1985 by Gildemeister

Peter Skene Ogden

Soon after the Hudson's Bay Company and the North West Company merged, Peter Skene Ogden was appointed Chief of the Snake Country Trapping Expedition. On December 20, 1824, Ogden and a formidable force of 71 men with 80 guns, 372 horses and 364 beaver traps set off from Flathead Post on Bull River (Montana) on the first Company trapping expedition. Their orders were to proceed to the heart of the Snake river country then swing south to the Rio Colorado, winter there and return up the west side of the Cascade Mountains to the Willamette river valley and finally to Fort Vancouver.

The journal of the first expedition was lost but it is known they camped in Bear Valley (Idaho) and while there a small group of American trappers set their camp alongside. They hoisted an American flag, openly passed a jug and called invitation to the freeman trappers among the Company men to join them.

Teton Mountains of Wyoming

A trapper of Ogden's era, Captain Benjamin Bonneville, described a freeman: *"They come and go, when and where they please; provide their own horses, arms, and other equipments; trap and trade on account, and dispose of their skins and peltries to the highest bidder....*

"The wandering whites who mingle for any length of time with the savages, have invariably a proneness to adopt savage habitudes; but none more so than the free trappers....You cannot pay a free trapper a greater compliment, than to persuade him you have mistaken him for an Indian brave; and, in truth, the counterfeit is complete. His hair, suffered to attain to a great length, is carefully combed out, and either left to fall carelessly over his shoulders, or plaited neatly and tied up in otter skins, or parti-colored ribbons. A hunting-shirt of ruffled calico of bright dyes, or of ornamented leather, falls to his knees; below which, curiously fashioned leggins, ornamented with strings, fringes, and a profusion of hawks' bells, reach to a costly pair of moccasins of the finest Indian fabric, richly embroidered with beads. A blanket of scarlet, or some other bright color, hangs from his shoulders, and is girt round his waist with a red sash, in which he bestows his pistols, knife, and the stem of his Indian pipe, preparations for peace or war...."

The freemen with Ogden were not actually freemen, their traps and outfits belonged to the Company and they had previously agreed to sell the furs they collected to the Company. But this did not keep 28 of them from deserting to the American camp which promised to pay eight times the going Company rate for beaver pelts, taking with them traps, outfits and furs.

The defections left Ogden's expedition undermanned. The exploration and trapping were cut short and Ogden returned to the Columbia across rivers he named Burnt River, Powder River and Grande Ronde River.

He arrived at Fort Nez Perce (also called Fort Walla Walla) and had twelve days rest before Dr. McLoughlin sent him on the second Snake river country trapping expedition.

Ft. Nez Perce on the Columbia River

The trappers traveled by horse following the Indian trail paralleling the Columbia until reaching River of the Falls (Deschutes River) where they turned south. Ogden wrote in his journal December 3, 1825: *"It is credible, altho we are yet so short a distance from the Columbia what a difference there is; soil rich; oak of a large size, abundant; grass green, weather warm; route hilly; high hills at a distance covered with snow...."*

December 5, 1825: *"A grand and noble sight — Mount Hood bearing due west, Mt. St. Helens and Mt. Nesqually [Mt. Adams] Northwest covered with eternal snow, and in a southern direction other lofty mountains in form and shape of sugar loves [loaves]. At the foot of all these mountains were lofty pnes [pines], which added greatly to the grandeur of the prospect...."*

As the expedition proceeded across the high desert paralleling the long Cascade range the weather turned cold. On December 30 Ogden wrote: *"My guide refuses to proceed; says there are no animals in the Snake Country, nor any beaver, and our horses will die; that we cannot cross the mountains. This is discouraging, but we must make a trail. On promising him a gun at Fort Nez Perces he consented to go."*

One week later he wrote: "*Many of the horses can scarcely crawl for want of grass, owing to frozen ground. March they must or we starve. We proceeded about five miles, encamped on a small fork lined with aspen. We are now on a very high land....The mountains [Blue Mountains] appeared about 30 miles distant, covered with snow and trees. They gave hope of red deer....*"

And on January 28: "*Our guide says there are 6 ft. of snow in mountains; impossible to pass in this direction; must try another. Many in the camp are starving. For the last ten days only one meal every two days. Still the company's horses must not fall a sacrifice. We hope when we are across the mountains to fare better; today 4 beaver.*"

The expedition crossed the divide from the head of the John Day River to the head of Burnt River. Ogden noted: "*Crossed river three times and found the ice sufficiently strong to bear our horses. One of the men detected this day stealing a beaver out of another man's trap; as starvation was the cause of this, he was pardoned on condition of promising not to do it again.*"

Hungry Horses

They camped on a river (Malheur River) and Ogden wrote February 14, 1826: *"We encamped on River au Malheur (unfortunate river) so called on account of property and furs having been hid here formerly, discovered and stolen by the natives...."*

February 16: *"Cold last night; very severe; rain froze; our prospects gloomy; we must continue to starve; now all are reduced to skin and bones; more beggarly looking beings I defy the world to produce. Still I have no cause to complain of the men; day after day they labor in quest of food and beaver without a shoe to their feet; the frozen ground is hardly comfortable; but it is an evil without remedy. The Snake Indians paid us a visit empty handed; they, too, complain of starvation. Were our horses in good condition, in 10 days we could make the buffalo ground. In their present weak state we cannot go in less than 25."*

The expedition reached a river (Owyhee River) which Ogden named Sandwich Island River in honor of two Hawaiians who were killed near the spot seven years earlier by Snake Indians.

March 13: *"Hunters arrived with 13 elk; never did men eat with better appetite; many did not stop to go to bed till midnight."*

And then on the following day: *"A Snake Indian of the plains informed us buffalo were near. I gave the call to start in pursuit and with the assistance of Indian horses, two buffalo were killed; our horses being too poor for buffalo running."*

They continued on to American Falls on the Snake River, trapping as they went, hunting and gathering roots to eat. On April 9, near the headwaters of the Snake, the expedition was surprised by the appearance of a party of Americans including many of the freemen who had deserted Ogden the previous year. Ogden wrote: *"If we were surprised then they were more so from an idea that the threats of last year would prevent us from returning to this quarter, but they find themselves mistaken; they camped a short distance away; all quiet."* The next day: *"Our deserters are already tired of their new masters and from their manner will soon return to us....I had a busy day settling with them, and more to my satisfaction and the company's than last year. We secured all the skins they had."*

They traveled to the vicinity of Raft River and the weather turned cold. Snow spit at them. May 6: *"Many of the trappers came in, almost froze, naked as the greater part are, and destitute of shoes, it is surprising not a murmur or complaint do I hear. Two-thirds without a blanket or any shelter, and have been so for the last six-months. Thirty-four beaver today."*

The expedition traveled west carrying 3,500 beaver pelts. Near a fork of the Owyhee River Ogden reported: *"The stones are as sharp as flints: our tracks could be followed by the blood from our horses' feet."* Not long after, the expedition divided with some of the men taking the furs to Fort Nez Perce while Ogden and the others crossed the headwaters of John Day River and blazed a trail over the Cascade Mountains to the Willamette Valley where they arrived in mid-July.

Picture Gorge of the John Day River

They canoed down the Willamette River and portaged around Willamette Falls. Ogden wrote: *"I suppose the height of the falls to be about 45 feet. We reached Fort Vancouver a little after sunset; received Dr. McLoughlin with every mark of attention. Distance from where I started this morning to Ft. Vancouver is 56 miles. With the exception of the falls not a ripple to be seen; a finer stream than the Willamette is not to be found; soil good; wood of all kinds in abundance; roots, elk, deer, salmon and sturgeon abundant; man could reside here and with but little industry enjoy every comfort. The distance from the ocean is 90 miles. No doubt ere many years a colony will be formed on the stream, and I am of opinion it will, with a little care, flourish, and settlers, by having a seaport so near them, with industry, might add greatly to their comforts and to their happiness. Thus ends my second trip and I am thankful for the many dangers I have escaped with all my party in safety. Had we not been obliged to kill our horses for food, the success of our expedition would have yielded handsome profits, as it is, fortunately, no loss will be sustained."*

Mt. Hood & Willamette River Dawn

Ogden rested for two months at Fort Vancouver before being sent on his third trapping expedition. This time, with 43 men, some women and children and over 100 head of horses, Ogden led the way south on an Indian trail along the Deschutes River. Upriver, at a point where the water ran frothy white over a ledge and funneled through a gap in a basalt flow, Ogden reported: "…*an Indian camp of 20 families. Finding a canoe also a bridge* [the original Sherars Bridge] *made of slender wood we began crossing, 5 horses were lost thro' the bridge. I am informed the salmon do not ascend beyond these falls.*"

October 5: "*We had certainly a most providential escape. Last night the Indians crossed the river* [Crooked River] *and set fire to the grass within 10 yards of our camp. The watch perceived it and gave the alarm. Had there not been a bunch of willows to arrest it everything would have been lost; a gale blowing at the time. This morning every Indian had decamped. If ever Indians deserve to be punished these do. They were well treated and fed by us and in return attempted to destroy us. This is Indian gratitude.*"

Crooked River Sunrise

By the end of October the expedition had passed through the Sylvaille (Silvies) river valley, an area rich with beaver, and descended to Salt Lake (Harney Lake). Here Ogden reported: *"An old woman camped with us the other night; and her information I have found most correct. From the severe weather last year, her people were reduced for want of food to subsist on the bodies of relations and children. She herself had not killed any one but had fed on two of her own children who died thro' weakness. Unfortunate creatures what privations you are doomed to endure; what an example for us at present reduced to one meal a day, how loudly and grievously we complain; when I consider the Snake [Indians] suffering compared to our own!"*

Ogden and his party traveled west. Ogden wrote: *"Swans numerous. Tho' 100 shots fired, not one killed....general gloom prevailing in camp, with all in a starving condition, so that plots are forming [among] the Freemen to separate. Should we not find animals our horses will fall to the kettle. I am at a loss how to act."*

The following day: *"Bad as prospects were yesterday they are worse to-day. It snowed all night and day. If this snow does not disappear our express men will never reach us. I hope they will not fall a prey to the Snakes. I intend to take the nearest route I can to discover to the Clammitte [Klamath] Country. My provisions and are fast decreasing. The hunters are discouraged. Day after day from morning to night in quest of animals; but not one track to they see."*

December 2 in the Klamath region Ogden noted: *"Late last night I was overjoyed by the arrival of one of my express men* [dispatched from Fort Vancouver]. *One of the men gone back in quest of horses discovered them, otherwise tho' the distance is only 4 miles, they would never have reached the camp. They could no longer walk or crawl. For 14 days they were without food; for 9 days without quenching thirst. Their horses were stolen on the River of the Falls by the Snakes."*

Christmas Day: *"I did not raise camp and we are reduced to one meal a day."* And on the first day of the new year, 1827: *"The men paid me their respects. I gave each a dram and tobacco. Goat killed."*

Traveling south to the Modoc nation in early February Ogden wrote: *"The Indians here have a contemptible opinion of all traders. Of the numerous murders and thefts committed, not one example has been made. Indians in general give us no credit for humanity, but attribute our not revenging murders to cowardice. When ever an opportunity offers of murder or theft, they allow it not to pass. I am of opinion if on first discovery of a strange tribe a dozen of them were shot, it would be the means of preserving many lives. Had this plan been adopted with the Snakes, they would not have been so daring and murdered 40 men. The same is the case with all Indians. Scripture gives us the right to retaliate in kind on those who murder. If men have means of preventing, why not put the means in execution. Why allow ourselves to be butchered and property stolen by such vile wretches who are not deserving to be numbered among the living the sooner dead the better."*

Swan

February 14: *"There is a moutain equal in height to Mount Hood or Vancouver, I have named Mt. Sastise [Mt. Shasta]."* By the end of February only 1,000 beaver pelts had been collected. Ogden, fearful the expedition might have to be abandoned, wrote on February 25: *"Should we not find beaver soon, starvation will make its appearance. We have only 2 mos. more but they are the most to be dreaded in the mountains. I wish they were past and our horses escaped from the kettle....One woman is so ill she must be tied on a horse. Nor can we afford her any relief. A sick person in this country is not only a burden to himself but to all; and the Canadians (freemen) are not overstocked with tender feelings."*

The trappers climbed into the mountains and near Siskiyou Divide, according to Ogden: *"The Indian guide saw a grizzly bear of large size, wh. the trappers fired at and wounded. The Indian requested the loan of a small axe with bow and arrows. Stripping himself naked, he rushed on the bear but paid dearly for his rashness. I do not suppose he will recover. He was injured in the head and lost one eye wh. was literally torn out. The bear remained in the bushes."*

The expedition returned to the Klamath region and crossed over to Harney Lake. June 1: *"I have no cause to complain of the conduct of the men, altho' obliged to subsist on horseflesh and scanty at that. Still the country must be explored as long as we find water or the means of advancing. Unfortunately this country has been too long neglected."*

Ogden ended his third expedition, returning to the Columbia in July 1827. In August, he embarked on his fourth expedition, this time to the upper Snake river region where during the season 3,000 beaver were taken.

Mt. Shasta from the Siskiyous

Ogden's fifth and last expedition, 1828-1829, took him through the open Owyhee country to the headwaters of the Humboldt River. By spring he had completed a big circle. While passing through the land of the Modoc Indians Ogden wrote on May 28, 1829: "*3 of the trappers came in with word of more traps stolen.* [They] *pursued the thieves and punished them but could not recover the traps. A man who had gone to explore the lake at this moment dashed in and gave the alarm of the enemy. He had a most narrow escape, only the fleetness of his horse saved his life. When rounding a point within sight of the lake, 20 men* [Indians] *on horse back gave the war cry. He fled. An Indian would have overtaken him, but he discharged his gun. He says the hills are covered with Indians. I gave orders to secure the horses, 10 men then started in advance to ascertain what the Indians were doing but not to risk a battle as we were too weak.* [In addition to Ogden there were only 14 men.] *They reported upwards of 200 Indians marching on our camp. They came on. Having signalled a spot for them about 500 yards from our camp, I desired them to be seated. This order was obeyed. From their dress and drums and the fact only one elderly man was with them, I concluded it was a war party. If they had not been discovered, they had intended to attack us, weak as we were in guns — only 12 — they would have been successful. It was a narrow escape.*"

The expedition set a return course along Sylvaille's River and over the Blue Mountains bound for Fort Nez Perce. They had taken over 3,500 beaver. The final entry in Ogden's journal is July 5: "*As the track to Nez Perce is now well known, and no danger to be apprehended, I shall to-morrow leave with 2 men for the fort. Thus ends my 5th trip to the Snake Country. We have no cause to complain of our returns.*"

Succor Creek of the Snake Country

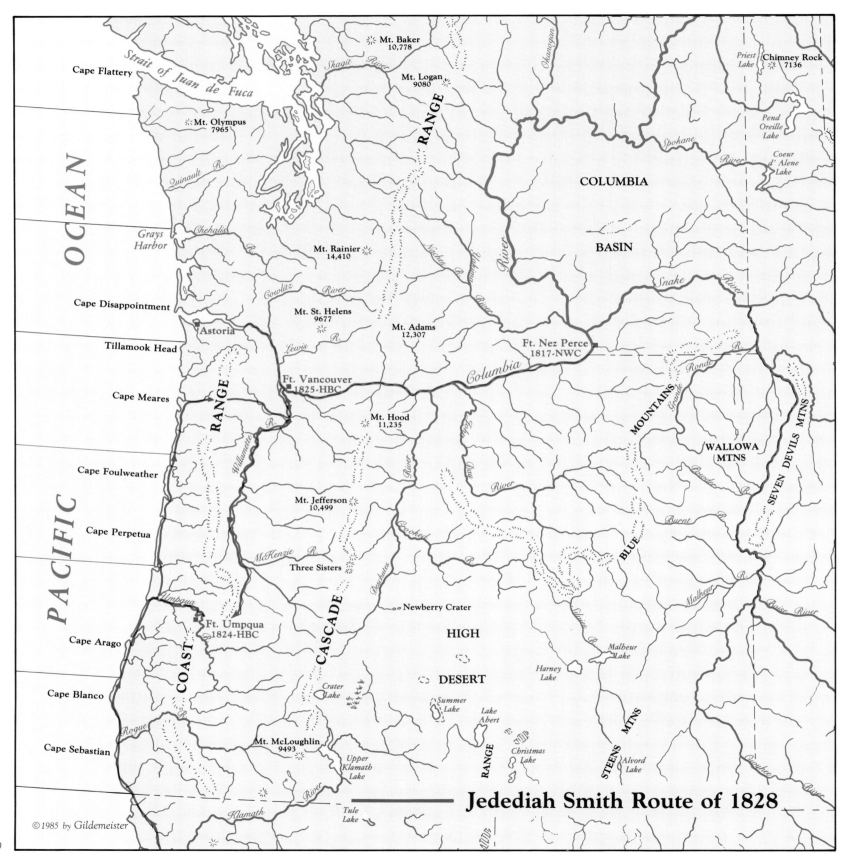

OCEAN

Strait of Juan de Fuca

Cape Flattery

Mt. Olympus
7965

Grays
Harbor

Chehalis

Quinault R.

Cape Disappointment

Tillamook Head

Astoria

Cape Meares

Cape Foulweather

Cape Perpetua

PACIFIC

Cape Arago

Cape Blanco

Cape Sebastian

Mt. Baker
10,778

Skagit River

Mt. Logan
9080

RANGE

Mt. Rainier
14,410

Cowlitz River

Mt. St. Helens
9677

Lewis R.

Mt. Adams
12,307

Naches R.

Yakima River

River

COLUMBIA

BASIN

Snake River

Priest
Lake

Chimney Rock
7136

Pend
Oreille
Lake

Spokane River

Coeur
d' Alene
Lake

Okanogan

Ft. Vancouver
1825·HBC

RANGE

Willamette R.

R.

Mt. Hood
11,235

Columbia

Ft. Nez Perce
1817-NWC

Grande Ronde

R.

MOUNTAINS

WALLOWA
MTNS

SEVEN DEVILS MTNS

Mt. Jefferson
10,499

McKenzie R.

Three Sisters

COAST

Ft. Umpqua
1824-HBC

Umpqua

Deschutes R.

River

Crooked R.

River

John Day

River

BLUE

Powder R.

Burnt R.

Malheur R.

Boise River

Newberry Crater

HIGH

CASCADE

DESERT

Harney
Lake

Malheur
Lake

Crater
Lake

Summer
Lake

Lake
Abert

Silvies R.

Mt. McLoughlin
9493

RANGE

Rogue R.

Upper
Klamath
Lake

Christmas
Lake

STEENS MTNS

Alvord
Lake

Owyhee River

Klamath River

Tule
Lake

Jedediah Smith Route of 1828

©1985 by Gildemeister

90

Jedediah Strong Smith

St. Louis was the fringe of civilization, a town of 5,000 where fine-clothed gentlemen rubbed shoulders with buckskin-clad mountain men and Indians. An advertisement appearing in the help wanted section of the **Missouri Gazette and Public Advertiser** on February 13, 1822, was addressed: *"To Enterprising Young men — The subscriber wishes to engage ONE HUNDRED MEN to ascend the River Missouri to its source, there to be employed for one, two or three years."*

Jedediah Strong Smith, a young man fresh from the Mohawk Valley of New York, arrived in St. Louis toting a Bible and an account of Lewis and Clark's expedition. He was seeking adventure and immediately was attracted by the advertisement. He signed on as a hunter and accompanied a band of William Ashley's mountain men into the Rocky Mountains.

In 1826 Smith, with David Jackson and William Sublette, bought out Ashley's interest and formed the Rocky Mountain Fur Company. That same year Smith led a party of trappers from the rendezvous grounds near the Great Salt Lake across the unexplored desert to the Spanish settlement at San Diego. Unfriendly officials advised Smith in strong terms that he should return immediately to American soil.

The expedition turned north and wasted precious time searching for a pass through the mountains. Heavy snow resisted any attempt at making a crossing, but Smith was determined. He left all but two men in winter camp and forced a route over the Sierra Nevada. Upon reaching the rendezvous grounds near Great Salt Lake Smith recruited a rescue party to return with him to California.

On the way Mojave Indians attacked and ten of the eighteen men were killed. And when the survivors reached California they were arrested by Spanish authorities and imprisoned. After a short stay they were released with the understanding they were banished from California and ordered to take the shortest route out of Spanish territory.

Smith was finally reunited with his men and they started east, but before crossing the mountains they veered north. They wintered on the American fork of the Sacramento River and in the spring continued north, trapping as they went. They angled to the coast hoping for better traveling

conditions but found short stretches of sandy beaches and long climbs over headlands where the trail clung precariously to vertical cliffs.

Smith kept a log of his travels. The last entry he made was July 4, 1828, between the Rogue and the Umpqua rivers: *"The traveling pretty bad, and as we were obliged to cross the low hills as they came in close to the beach and the beach being so bad that we could not get along, thickety and timbered and some bad ravines to cross. We enc. on a long point where there was but little grass for the horses. Good deal of elk signs, and several hunters out killed nothing, the weather still good."*

Harrison Rogers, second in command, also maintained a journal and on July 12, near the mouth of the Umpqua River, he penned: *"We commenced crossing the river early and had our goods and horses over by 8 o.c. then packed up and started a N.E. course up the river and traveled 3 mi and enc. Had several Inds. along; one of the Inds. stole an ax and we were obliged to seize him before we could scare him to make him give it up. Capt. Smith and one of them caught him and put a cord around his neck, and the rest of us stood with our guns ready in case they made resistance there was about 50 inds present but did not pretend to resist tying the other."*

The axe, which had been buried in sand, was returned and the Indian released. Unknown to the Americans they had embarrassed and humbled a chief of the Kelawatset tribe. He called his braves into a war council and urged them to fall on the white strangers and wipe out memory of his shame. At first the others refused but in time they were convinced the Americans must be slain.

The morning of July 14 Smith was up early, as was his custom, to scout the beginnings of the trail they would take that day. He headed up the Smith River in a canoe with Richard Leland and a native guide to look for a suitable place to cross the horses. Before setting out Smith warned Harrison Rogers not to allow the gathering crowd of Indians into camp. Rogers disobeyed with tragic consequence.

The atmosphere in the American camp was relaxed. Men sat cleaning rifles or eating. None were prepared for action. A piercing whoop brought movement. Knives and hatchets the Indians had hidden under blankets came into view and the savages fell on the white men. Some of the Americans were killed right where they sat, others tried to gain their feet and were quickly struck down. Fiendish shouts mingled with the dying groans of the white men as the Kelawatsets began looting packs, taking supplies and beaver pelts. Only two Americans survived. Arthur Black darted into the woods and outran the Indians, and John Turner fought his way through, brandishing a fire brand until he could dive into the river.

Smith and Leland were returning very near camp when the Indian guide intentionally flipped the canoe and swam away. Other Indians along the bank shot arrows at the two men struggling in the water. Smith and Leland swam underwater, coming up only for breaths of air, to the opposite shore. They ran into the woods in different directions. Smith sought high ground overlooking the camp and what he saw sickened him. The savages were mutilating the bodies of his men. He knew he was on his own, and the closest white settlement, the Hudson's Bay post at Vancouver, was 150 miles north.

Coastal Dune Morning

Sun and blue sky bathed Fort Vancouver in summer. In the twilight of August 7, as the sun set on the Pacific, the gates to the fort were drawn shut and locked. After dark came a tremendous uproar from outside. Chief Factor McLoughlin was called for. He came to the gate and discovered a party of Indians with a white man so weak he could hardly stand.

It was Arthur Black. Later, when he could talk, he told Dr. McLoughlin the harrowing story of his escape. He said he was the only survivor of an expedition of the Rocky Mountain Fur Company headed by Jedediah Smith, and that during the attack he was on the outskirts of the camp. At the initial blood-curdling whoop he sprang into action. Three Indians jumped upon him but he shook them off, fired one quick shot into the mass of Indians and dashed into the woods. The Indians searched for him but were distracted by the spoils back at camp.

Rather than stick to the main Indian trail up the Willamette Valley, Black went straight north through the mountains. He wandered for weeks existing on a few berries until he came upon an Indian village. He was in such an exhausted state he turned himself over to them. They were Killamoux (Tillamooks), a tribe friendly with the traders of Hudson's Bay Company. They escorted him to Fort Vancouver.

Dr. McLoughlin was generous with the Indians and, thinking others might have escaped, sent runners to various Willamette chiefs giving them gifts of tobacco and requesting they search the valley for any American trappers. With the gifts was the warning that if the trappers were ill-treated the Indians would be punished.

A brigade under the command of Alexander McLeod had been forming to trade and trap along the coast south of the Columbia River and Dr. McLoughlin ordered them to begin a search for survivors of the massacre on the Umpqua River. Before they could depart three white men — Smith, Leland and Turner — stumbled in together. According to one account they were: *"Bareheaded and barefooted, more nearly dead then alive, they had endured on roots and the creeping things of the forest."*

The brigade, 38 Company men and Indians, left the fort September 6, 1828. Accompanying them were the four American trappers who wanted revenge on the Kelawatsets and to get back the furs they had spent two years accumulating.

Ascending the Willamette the brigade met Michel LaFramboise, a freeman, coming from the south. He reported that the Umpqua region was in turmoil. Other tribes were threatening war with the Kelawatsets for the killings. The personal property and furs of the Americans were scattered up and down the coast.

LaFramboise delivered the same message to Dr. McLoughlin who responded to McLeod: *"I...am extremely sorry to find that Mr. Smith's affair has a more gloomy appearance than I expected and it seems to be in that state either that we must make war on the murderers of his people to make them restore his property or drop the business entirely.*

"I know many people will argue that we have no right to make war on the natives; on the other hand if the business be dropped, will not our personal security be endangered whatever this report reaches? Again suppose that by accident a vessel was wrecked on the coast; to possess themselves of the property would not the natives seeing these murderers escape with impunity kill all the crew that fell in their power and say as these now do, 'We did not take them to be the same people as you'?...is it not our duty as Christians to endeavor as much as possible to prevent the perpetration of such atrocious crimes? And is there any measure so likely to accomplish so effectually this object as to make these murderers restore at least, the ill-gotten booty now in their possession?"

On October 11 the brigade reached the Umpqua River. As they approached, the Indians fled. A messenger was sent to inform them they were in no danger, that the white man was not seeking to punish them. The following day the Umpqua chief Starnoose and his followers came to camp with eight of the Americans' horses. Starnoose said they had been obtained from the Kelawatset tribe.

Starnoose accompanied the McLeod party and the four Americans down the Umpqua River. At each village the Indians were induced to surrender the loot they had obtained in trade from the Kelawatsets — beaver and otter skins, rifles, pistols, traps, kettles, trade beads, clothing, maps and horses.

At the confluence of Smith River and the Umpqua River the expedition came upon the grisly scene of the massacre. Human skeletons picked clean by animals and birds were scattered in the sun. They buried the bones and continued, stopping at Indian villages gathering skins, goods and horses and restoring them to the American owners. Near Ten-Mile Creek the Indians turned over the journals of Smith and Harrison Rogers. After acquiring these, the men returned to Fort Vancouver.

The following spring, 1829, Smith and Arthur Black parted Fort Vancouver after selling their furs to the Hudson's Bay Company. They traveled east and were reunited with the other partners of the Rocky Mountain Fur Company at rendezvous in Pierre's Hole, a beautiful valley in the shadow of the Tetons. They were never to return to the Oregon country.

For three years Smith had wandered west of the Rockies. Of the 32 men who shared in his adventures, 25 were killed by Indians. Smith, only 31 years old, had become one of the greatest western explorers, the first American to reach California overland and the first to traverse the length of California and Oregon by land.

Coastal Mountains

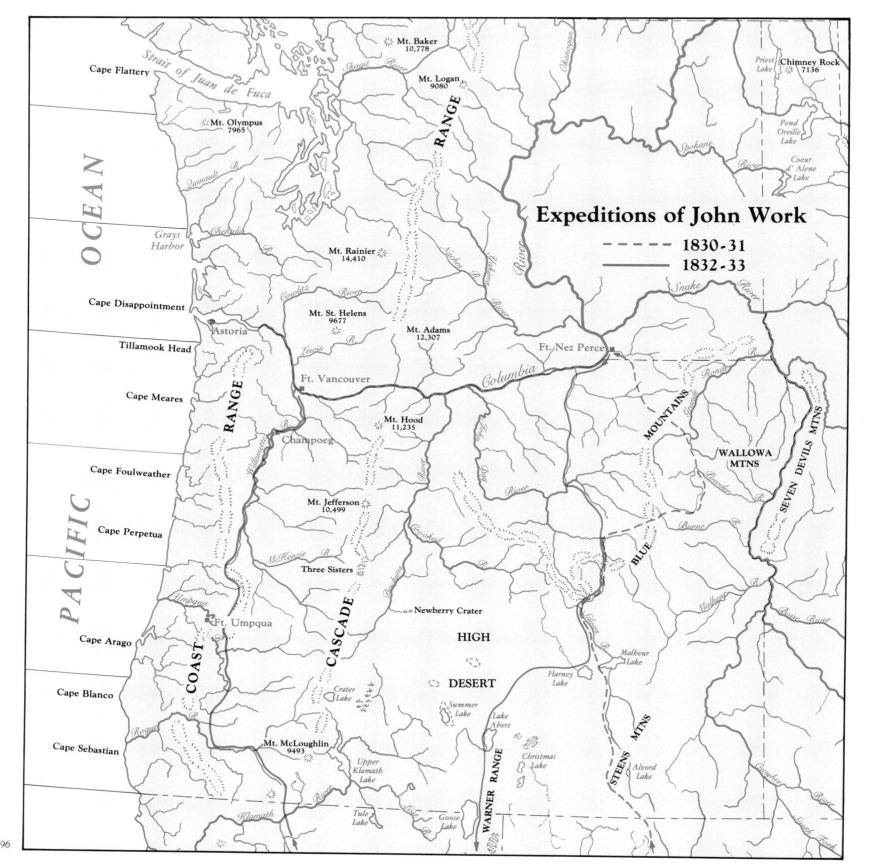

Expeditions of John Work

- - - - - 1830-31
———— 1832-33

Cape Flattery
Strait of Juan de Fuca
Mt. Baker
10,778
Skagit River
Mt. Logan
9080
RANGE
Okanogan
Priest Lake
Chimney Rock
7136
Pend Oreille Lake
Mt. Olympus
7965
Spokane
Coeur d' Alene Lake
OCEAN
Quinault R.
River
Chehalis
Grays Harbor
Mt. Rainier
14,410
Naches R.
Yakima R.
River
Snake
River
Cape Disappointment
Cowlitz
River
Mt. St. Helens
9677
Astoria
Mt. Adams
12,307
Ft. Nez Perce
Tillamook Head
Lewis R.
Columbia
Grande Ronde
Cape Meares
Ft. Vancouver
PACIFIC
RANGE
R.
Champoeg
Mt. Hood
11,235
John Day River
Powder R.
WALLOWA MTNS
MOUNTAINS
SEVEN DEVILS MTNS
Cape Foulweather
Willamette
Cape Perpetua
McKenzie R.
Mt. Jefferson
10,499
River
Crooked
River
Burnt R.
COAST
Three Sisters
CASCADE
Deschutes R.
BLUE
Malheur
Boise River
Newberry Crater
Malheur Lake
Cape Arago
Ft. Umpqua
Umpqua
HIGH
Harney Lake
Silvies R.
Cape Blanco
Crater Lake
Summer Lake
DESERT
Malheur Lake
Owyhee River
South Fork
Cape Sebastian
Rogue R.
Mt. McLoughlin
9493
Upper Klamath Lake
River
Christmas Lake
Lake Abert
STEENS MTNS
Alvord Lake
WARNER RANGE
Klamath
Tule Lake
Lost R.
Goose Lake

96

John Work

John Work came west with the Hudson's Bay Company in 1823 and began a seven-year hitch as a Company trapper and trader out of forts on the upper Columbia — Spokane House, Flathead and Kootenai. He was in charge of transferring the stock and materials from Fort George to Fort Vancouver when it was built and oversaw construction of Fort Colville. In 1830 he was promoted to Chief Trader, succeeding Peter Skene Ogden as head of the Snake Country Trapping Expeditions.

Work led the expedition of 1830-1831 south as far as the Great Salt Lake Divide. Swinging west they retraced the route taken by Ogden and trapped on Ogden's River (Humboldt River) for nearly a month before turning north.

Storm over Pueblo Valley

Along the Owyhee River Work wrote in his journal June 19, 1831: *"The river is still full to the banks and all the low plains overflowed. The men again visited the river but could not put a trap in the water. Both people and horses are like to be devoured by innumerable swarms of mosquitoes and sand flies. The horses cannot feed they are so much annoyed by them, the banks of the river are so swampy that they bog when they approach to drink."*

June 20: *"...Two of the men, J. Toupe and G. Rocque, killed a horse having nothing to eat, the provisions being all done....This is really a miserable, poor country, not even an antelope to be seen."*

June 25: *"Marched seven miles along the foot of the mountain, and 15 miles across the plain to a little river which runs to the southward, and which we found impassable, its banks having been lately overflowed, and remain still like a quagmire. The best hunters are out, but as usual did not see a single animal of any sort. One of the men was under the necessity of killing one of his horses to eat. Thus are the people in this miserable country obliged to kill and feed upon these useful animals, the companions of their labors. We passed a small Indian camp, but the poor, frightened wretches fled on our appearance and concealed themselves among the wormwood."*

Sheepshead Mountains

July 2: "*Continued our journey 19 miles to Sylvalle's Lake* [Malheur Lake]. *The road part of the day stony. The lake is unusually high, and the water brackish and so very bad that it is like a vomit to drink it. The hunters were out but without success. There are a number of wild fowl in the lake, but they are so shy that they cannot be approached.*"

July 5: "*Did not raise camp in order to allow the horses to repose, of which they are in much need, they having marched 19 days successively without stopping a day to rest. They have been becoming lean for some time back and their hoofs are so much worn that some of them are becoming lame....*"

July 6: "*...In the morning one of the men arrived with a load of young herons, he found a place where they were very numerous. Some more of the people who are short of food immediately went to get a supply. These birds are very fat. Some of the people say they are very good, others say that they are scarcely eatable.*"

July 10: "*Crossed the mountains to Day's River* [John Day River], *a distance of 22 miles. The road very hilly and steep, particularly the N. side of the mountain. The mountain is thickly wooded with tall pine timber. Both people and horses much fatigued on nearing the camp, part of the road stony. Day's River is well wooded with poplar and willows. Two Indians visited our camp this morning and traded five beaver.*"

Harney Basin Sundown

July 12: "*Continued our route down the river, which still runs to the westward 11 miles, when we stopped near a camp of Snake Indians who have the river barred across for the purpose of catching salmon. We, with difficulty, obtained a few salmon from them, perhaps enough to give all hands a meal. They are taking very few salmon, and are complaining of being hungry themselves. No roots can be obtained from them, but some of the men traded [for] two or three dogs, but even the few of these animals they have are very lean, a sure sign of a scarcity of food among Indians....*"

July 17: "*Continued our journey across the mountains 25 miles. The country the same in appearance as yesterday until we got out of the woods in the after part of the day, when the road lay over a number of naked stony hills [southwest of the Umatilla River]. The length of the day's journey and the badness of the road rendered this a harassing day both on men and horses. Some fresh tracks of red deer were seen in the course of the day, but they could not be come up with.*"

July 18: "*Proceeded ahead of the camp early in the morning accompanied by seven men and arrived at Fort Nezperces in the afternoon. Mainly through there being soft sand during the heat of the day was excessively oppressive on the horses as well as the riders.*"

July 20: "*Since our spring journey commenced we have traveled upwards of 1000 miles, and from the height of the water and the scarcity of beaver we have very little for the labor and trouble which we experience. Previous to taking up our winter quarters last fall we traveled upwards of 980 miles, which, with the different moves made during the winter makes better than 2000 miles traveled during our voyage....Total loss of horses during the voyage, 82....*"

Before embarking on the next expedition, Work penned a letter to his friend Edward Ermatinger: "*I am going to start with my ragamuffin freemen to the southward towards the Spanish settlements but with what success I cannot say. I am tired of the cursed country, Ned, and becoming more dissatisfied every day with the measures in it; things don't go fair, I don't think I shall remain long, my plan is to hide myself in some out of the way corner, and drag out the remainder of my days as quietly as possible. Susette [his half-breed Indian wife] is well, we have now got three little girls, they accompanied me these last two years, but I leave them behind this one, the misery is too great. I shall be very lonely without them but the cursed trip exposes them to too much hardship.*"

Silvies Valley & the Strawberry Mountains

The band of trappers, numbering 100 men, women and children, departed Fort Walla Walla on September 6, 1832, and crossed south over the Blue Mountains. They reached the headwaters of Silvies River which they followed to its mouth at Malheur Lake. They swung west across the sagebrush desert finding their way by landmark buttes. Bending southwest they skirted an alkali lake Ogden named Salt Lake (Lake Abert), and at last reached the southern boundary of Oregon country. The party crossed the mountains near Lassen Peak and continued south to the Bonaventura Valley (Sacramento Valley).

In the early years of the 19th century, the great valley of California formed by the Sacramento and San Joaquin rivers was a no man's land traversed by wandering Russians, British and Americans. Glimpses of these early explorers flash across the pages of John Work's journals in his brief descriptions of the competition to be first to harvest the streams for beaver and other fur-bearing animals.

The Work expedition wintered near the Sacramento River. Their stay was marked by belligerent Indians, a scarcity of furs and the plentiful mosquitoes which brought fever and sickness with their bites. In the spring, sick and weakened, they visited the Bay of San Francisco before heading north.

September 15, 1833: *"Raised camp and proceeded about 9 miles to the foot of the Mountain [Mt. Shasta] and encamped at a small creek with little more than enough of water for the people and scarcely any for their horses. — We passed a much better encampment, but did not know it at the time. — The sick continued much the same, Some of them who are badly clothed and ill provided with the means of sheltering themselves feel much inconvenienced from the cold weather. — "*

September 17: *"Sharp frost in the morning stormy weather during the day. — We were deterred from raising camp on account of C. Groslui dieing just as the people were catching the horses. — This poor man has left a widow & 6 children to lament his loss & all ill with the fever except one child; he had nearly recovered himself, and imprudently exerted himself too much & exposed himself to the water, which occasioned a relapse when he became worse than at first, for some days he refused all sustenance, and had to be carried on a kind of litter on horseback. There was little expectation of his recovery but it was not supposed he would die so suddenly. — The rest of our sick people continue in much the same condition. — "*

September 22: *"The Indians here [near Rogue River] bear a very bad character, during the first watch last night a party of them came to the other side of the river opposite to us and made a large fire and raised the war cry. I was in a paroxysm of the fever & could not stir out. Some of the people said that there were a great many of them & others that there were but a few. Owing to our helpless state, there being only 15 men in health in the camp, I felt uneasy for some time. All the people who were able were ordered to arms the Indians in a short time went off and we saw or heard no more of them."*

September 26: *"One of the men P. Bernie died during the first watch last night, he had been for a length of time so weak that he had to be tied on his horse, for some days back he had become so feeble, that there was little hopes of his recovery, but it was not expected that he would die so suddenly, yet, he had anticipated death himself and had arranged his little affairs, he had for some time little or no sustenance, so that his strength became exhausted, he has left a wife and 5 children, all ill with the fever. The people are getting more discouraged every day. — We were deterred from raising camp on account of one of the women A. Longtain's wife being so ill that she was not expected to live out the day. — The hunters were out but without success. — "*

October 8: *"Continued our journey across a point and fell upon the north or principal fork of the Umpquah [Umpqua River] which we crossed immediately and encamped on its North Bank. — Some of the sick particularly the children who were first taken ill are recovering....The others still continue very ill, some of them I fear will not live to reach the fort. I am rendered so weak that I am with difficulty able to make the days journey short as they mostly are, for some days I have had no shaking fits, but the hot fever visited me regularly. I am again attacked with the trembling fits. — "*

October 13: *"M. LaFramboise accompanied by four men and some Indians arrived from Ft. Vancouver.... He informs me that owing to false reports which have reached Mr. C.F. [Chief Factor] McLoughlin he is very anxious for the safety of our party, I have written a letter to apprise him of our situation and cause of our delay...."*

October 18: *"...Late in the evening the Indian who returned on the morning of the 14th, with the letter for Mr. C.F. McLoughlin, arrived on his return from Vancouver, he brought a letter from Mr. C.F. McLoughlin, together with a supply of tea & Sugar & Some bread & butter, which is very acceptable to me in my present feeble state. — "*

October 19: *"Continued our journey 15 miles to Yamhill river.... This was a severe day on the weakest of the sick people Some of them did not reach the encampment till after dark."*

October 20: *"Heavy rain all day. — The bad weather deterred us from raising camp. — "*

October 21: *"Rained the greater part of the day. — Did not raise camp, being unwilling to expose our sick people to the wet. — The most of the sick people are recovering fast. — "*

October 22: *"Stormy with excessive heavy rain all day. — The river is rising fast. — Did not raise camp, on account of the heavy rain our temporary shelters are scarcely habitable. — "*

October 23: *"Fair weather in the morning, but rain the most of the day afterwards, — The river had rose to such a height that we could not cross it but with canoes or rafts.... This was a very unfavourable day for the sick as we were exposed to a good deal of heavy rain. — "*

October 24: *"As it was very bad landing it was noon by the time the baggage was got all across the river, we nevertheless raised camp and proceeded on to Sand encampment [Champoeg] where we arrived late in the evening. — I borrowed a canoe from one of the settlers Bt. McKay to take down the river...."*

October 26: *"The people proceeded by land, and I embarked in the canoe which I borrowed from Bt. McKay with two Indians which were hired for the purpose, and descended the river but the Indians were such poor workers that the people arrived at the river of the Chutes [Willamette Falls] a little before me...."*

October 27: *"Had the remainder of the baggage crossed in the morning when we advanced to the Chutes where we encamped, The people were afterwards employed, drying and beating their furs. — "*

October 28: *"Sent off all the healthy men with the horses to put them on the island at the entrance of the Willamut, and to bring up the boats which are waiting us at the little Channel, to take on the people and the baggage to the fort. After much difficulty I hired a canoe from the Indians, & two indians and started myself for the fort, by water; the Indians became fatigued towards evening and I encamped a little above the island. — Shortly after leaving the camp I met a boat with four men coming to meet us. I directed the boat to go on and take in a load of baggage and people and return to the fort immediately. — "*

October 29: *"Embarked at daylight and arrived at the fort by 9 o'clock, where I was received with a hearty welcome...."*

October 31: *"The other two boats arrived at the fort with the rest of the people and baggage. — The people who were sick are so far recovered, that but a few of them require to go under the Doctors care but they were so much exhausted and continue still so debilitated that it will be some time before they be fit for any duty. Several times during our journey, the people were so weak that I was apprehensive the greater part of them would die on the way before reaching the fort, I attribute their recovery in a great measure to the change of climate in the Mountains, but as this had not an immediate effect they did not begin to get better until some time after we crossed the mountains."*

Work remained at Fort Vancouver recovering from his illness for many months. He led his last expedition in 1834 to the Umpqua River and back. Later that year he was placed in charge of shipping on the Columbia River and held that position for three years before accepting the assignment to command Fort Simpson.

In February 1840 John Tod wrote a letter to Edward Ermatinger concerning their mutual friend John Work: *"Friend Work on his way to Vanc'r last fall was induced to remain here with me two nights during which many a phillipic was held forth on the privations of the Service and this 'Cursed Country,' but he is as far as ever from coming to any determination about quitting it. You would scarcely know him he is quite bald and altogether has really an old appearance, in short he goes under the name here of 'Old Gentleman'."*

Another letter from Tod to Ermatinger, this dated November 1861, stated: *"You will be sorry to hear of the long protracted suffering of our friend Work — he has scarcely been out of bed for the past two months — his complaint is a relapse of fever and ague with which he was attacked at Vancouver 27 years ago....Latterly he has become so much reduced, and so very weak I have felt it a sacred duty to be constantly with him, administering what little consolation to him I can — it has been no small gratification to myself to think I may have been of some use to him in what I greatly fear may be amoung his last days....I left him only a few hours since I told him it was for the purpose of writing to You, as soon as your name was mentioned, the poor sufferer struggled hard to get up — 'Yes do,' said he, 'and tell him oh tell him that I shall never again see him in this world.' "*

Two days before Christmas 1861 Tod penned: *"I have just returned from the house of mourning where lays the body of our departed friend Work...."*

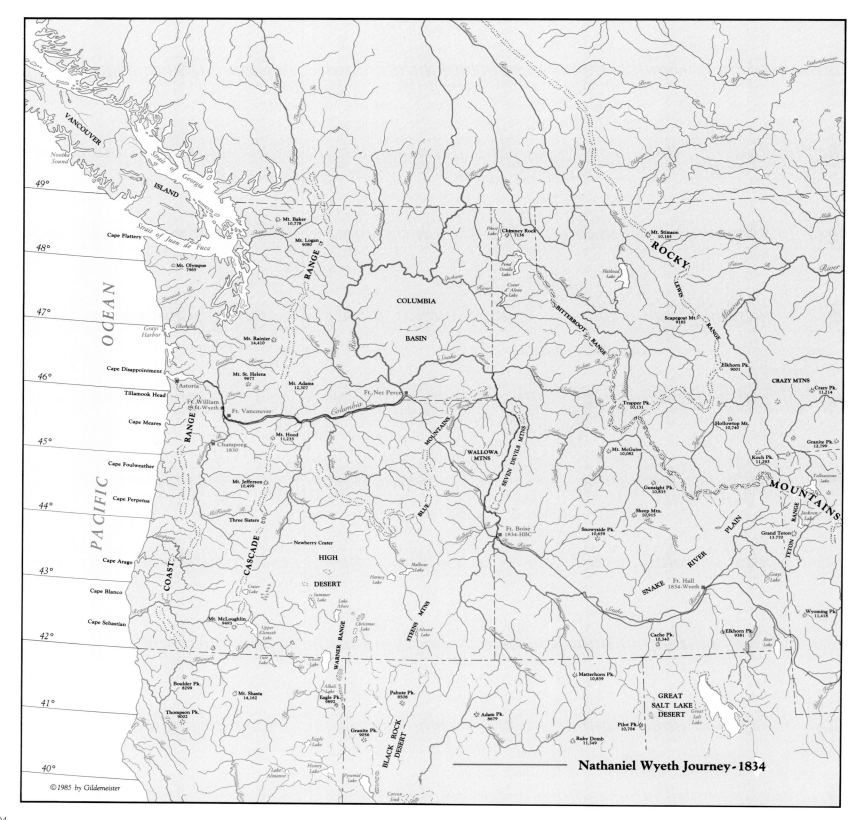

VANCOUVER
ISLAND

Nootka
Sound

Cape Flattery

Strait of Georgia

Strait of Juan de Fuca

PACIFIC OCEAN

Grays Harbor

Cape Disappointment

Tillamook Head

Cape Meares

Cape Foulweather

Cape Perpetua

Cape Arago

Cape Blanco

Cape Sebastian

COAST RANGE

CASCADE RANGE

49°
48°
47°
46°
45°
44°
43°
42°
41°
40°

☀ Mt. Baker
10,778

Mt. Logan
9080

☀ Mt. Olympus
7965

Mt. Rainier
14,410

Mt. St. Helens
9677

Mt. Adams
12,307

☀ Astoria
Ft. William
1834-Wyeth
Ft. Vancouver

☀ Mt. Hood
11,235

Champoeg
1830

Mt. Jefferson
10,499

Three Sisters

Newberry Crater

Crater Lake

Mt. McLoughlin
9493

Upper
Klamath
Lake

Tule
Lake

Mt. Shasta
14,162

Boulder Pk.
8299

Thompson Pk.
9002

Granite Pk.
9056

Eagle
Lake

Honey
Lake

Lake
Almanor

Pyramid
Lake

Carson
Sink

BLACK ROCK DESERT

WARNER RANGE

Goose
Lake

Alkali
Lake

Eagle Pk.
9892

Summer
Lake

Lake
Abert

Christmas
Lake

Harney
Lake

Malheur
Lake

STEENS MTNS

Alvord
Lake

HIGH DESERT

BLUE MOUNTAINS

WALLOWA MTNS

SEVEN DEVILS MTNS

Ft. Nez Perce

Columbia River

COLUMBIA BASIN

Snake River

Ft. Boise
1834-HBC

Pahute Pk.
8508

Adam Pk.
8679

Matterhorn Pk.
10,839

Ft. Hall
1834-Wyeth

SNAKE RIVER PLAIN

Ruby Domb
11,349

Pilot Pk.
10,704

Cache Pk.
10,340

Elkhorn Pk.
9381

Wyoming Pk.
11,418

GREAT SALT LAKE DESERT

Great
Salt
Lake

Bear
Lake

Grays
Lake

TETON RANGE

Grand Teton
13,770

Jackson
Lake

Yellowstone
Lake

ROCKY MOUNTAINS

Mt. Stimson
10,165

Flathead
Lake

LEWIS RANGE

Scapegoat Mt.
9185

BITTERROOT RANGE

Priest
Lake

Pend
Oreille
Lake

Coeur
d'Alene
Lake

Chimney Rock
7136

Elkhorn Pk.
9001

CRAZY MTNS

Crazy Pk.
11,214

Hollowtop Mt.
10,740

Granite Pk.
12,799

Koch Pk.
11,293

Trapper Pk.
10,131

Mt. McGuire
10,082

Gunsight Pk.
10,835

Sheep Mtn.
10,915

Snowside Pk.
10,659

Missouri River

Columbia River

Saskatchewan

☐☐☐ Nathaniel Wyeth Journey - 1834

© 1985 by Gildemeister

104

Nathaniel J. Wyeth

From a comfortable chair in Boston, Nathaniel Wyeth read published reports of American fur traders in the West and decided that he, too, should get in on the chance to make a fortune. Like Astor, he planned to establish a main trading post accessible from the sea and outposts scattered throughout the Columbia drainage. He would meet the mighty Hudson's Bay Company head to head.

Wyeth also researched the method of curing and packing salmon for export and the cultivation of tobacco with an eye toward the Indian trade. He had little capital of his own but convinced friends and acquaintances to join him in a joint stock company.

Wyeth chartered the small vessel *Sultana*, loaded her with supplies and trade goods and sent her around the Horn to the Columbia. He planned to lead an overland expedition and meet her when she arrived. May 11, 1832, in the company of 20 men, Wyeth departed Boston. He met William Sublette at Independence, Missouri, and fell in with him to the rendezvous at Pierre's Hole.

At the rendezvous, trappers discussed how trapping in the Rocky Mountains was every bit as good as Oregon without as many dangers. Several of Wyeth's men approached him and asked for a meeting to give every freeman a chance to speak his sentiment and a choice to continue or join the other trappers in the Rockies.

Teton Mountains of Upper Snake River

Wyeth stated that as long as he remained in charge of the expedition no vote would be allowed. If his men deserted he would go on alone. He ordered the roll be called and the clerk asked each man if he wished to quit or continue. The clerk called 18 names; seven elected to quit and eleven declared, *"Going on!"*

They departed Pierre's Hole on July 17 and did not reach the lower Columbia until the 8th of November. It was with bitter disappointment they learned the *Sultana*, their supply ship, had been wrecked and her cargo lost. Wyeth wrote in his journal: *"...my men came forward and unanimously desired to be released from their engagement with the view to returning home as soon as possible and for that end to remain here and work for a maintenance until an opportunity should occur. I could not refuse, they had already suffered much and our number was so small that the prospect of remuneration to them was very small. I have therefore no men...."*

After traveling across the country only one member of the Wyeth expedition felt compelled to view the Pacific Ocean. John Ball wrote: *"I urged the men to go with me, but all declined. So I went alone to look at the broad Pacific, with nothing between me and Japan. Standing on the brink of the great Pacific with the waves washing my feet was the happiest hour of my long journey. There I watched until the sun sank beneath the water. Then, by the light of the moon, I returned to camp, feeling I had not crossed the continent in vain."*

After visiting Fort Vancouver, Ball entered in his journal: *"Mr. Wyeth and myself were invited by Doctor McLoughlin, the oldest partner and nominal governor, to his own table and rooms at the fort. Others were quartered out of the fort. I soon gave Doctor McLoughlin and Captain Wyeth to understand that I was on my own hook, and had no further connection with the party. We were received with the greatest kindness as guests, which was very acceptable, or else we would have had to hunt for subsistence. But not liking to live gratis, I asked the doctor for some employment. He repeatedly answered me that I was a guest and not expected to work. But after much urging, he said if I was willing he would like me to teach his own son and the other boys in the fort, of whom there were a dozen. Of course, I gladly accepted the offer. So the boys were sent to my room to be instructed. All were half-breeds, as there was not a white woman in Oregon....I found the boys docile and attentive and they made good progress. The doctor often came into the school, and was well satisfied and pleased. One day he said: 'Ball, anyway, you will have the reputation of teaching the first school in Oregon.' So, I passed the winter of 1832 and 1833."*

In February 1833 Wyeth and two of his men, Wiggin Abbott and John Woodman, departed Fort Vancouver headed overland for Boston. Although his first undertaking had been a failure and the investment lost, Wyeth reasoned he had gained experience and knowledge of the country. He arrived in Boston in November and immediately called a meeting of investors.

Wyeth laid out the opportunities he had seen, hoping to persuade his associates to continue their financial support. He held a contract to deliver $3,000 worth of supplies to the rendezvous for the Rocky Mountain Fur Company. He stated the Oregon country possessed untapped resources in fur that could not be singly claimed by the Hudson's Bay Company. As an added inducement he unveiled a plan to pack and export what seemed to be an unlimited supply of salmon.

Backers were sufficiently impressed with Wyeth's presentation that they agreed to finance a second expedition. The Columbia River Fishing and Trade Company was organized and the ship *May Dacre* outfitted. Wyeth struck out for St. Louis to recruit 70 men.

In addition to purveying supplies to Sublette at the rendezvous, Wyeth agreed to guide a small group of American missionaries led by Jason Lee to the Oregon country. He was forced to wait in Independence, Missouri, for these missionaries and he wrote impatiently: *"There are none of the Dignitaries with me as yet, and if they 'preach' much longer in the States they will lose their passage, for I will not wait a minute for them."*

The missionaries arrived and the long journey was begun April 28, 1834. They reached South Pass in mid-June and met with representatives of the Rocky Mountain Fur Company. A disagreement arose and the company refused to accept the goods they had contracted to buy. Wyeth found himself compelled to dispose of his merchandise directly to the trappers and Indians. Two hundred miles beyond the point of rendezvous (40 miles northeast of today's Pocatello, Idaho, on the Snake River), Wyeth constructed a trading post. He remained there nearly a month to insure it could be easily defended by a minimum of men.

Wyeth wrote: *"I have built a fort on Snake, or Lewis River, which I named Fort Hall from the oldest gentleman in the concern. We manufactured a magnificent flag from some unbleached sheeting, a little red flannel and a few blue patches, saluted it with damaged powder and wet it in vilanous alcohol, and after all it makes, I do assure you, a very respectable appearance amid the dry and desolate regions of central America....After building this fort I sent messengers to the neighboring nations to induce them to come to it to trade."*

The expedition split into smaller groups. Some trapped or traded, others stayed at Fort Hall and Wyeth and his group — the missionaries had gone on ahead — resumed their march for the Columbia. They reached their goal September 14, 1834, one day in advance of the *May Dacre*.

Another trading post was established on Wapato Island (Sauvie Island) at the mouth of the Willamette River and named Fort William in honor of one of Wyeth's investors. Houses, a blacksmith shop and a wood shop were built. Land was cleared and in the spring planted to a variety of crops. It was fertile land, the site of a permanent Indian camp for centuries until an epidemic brought by the earliest white men destroyed the Indian population.

Wyeth wrote of the area: *"This Wapato island....consists of woodlands and prairie, and on it there is considerable deer, and those who could spare time to hunt might live well, but mortality has carried off to a man its inhabitants, and there is nothing to attest that they ever existed except their decaying houses, their graves and their unburied bones, of which there are heaps. So you see, as the righteous people of New England say, providence has made room for me, and without doing them more injury than I should if I had made room for myself, viz., killing them off."*

Wyeth hoped the salmon packing plant would be profitable but like his other enterprises it, too, proved a failure. Because of the epidemic there were few Indian workers to catch the salmon, and then the white men began to suffer. Even Wyeth became ill. He wrote: *"I am now little better from a severe attack of bilious fever. I did not expect to recover, and am still a wreck, and the sick list has been usually one-third of the whole number, and the rest much frightened. Thirteen deaths have occurred....Our salmon fishing has not succeeded; half a cargo only was obtained. Our people are sick and die off like rotten sheep, of bilious disorders."*

John McLoughlin felt the Hudson's Bay Company was obliged to eliminate the competition of the American trading post on the lower Columbia. A rival post was opened across the river from Fort William where prices for goods and supplies undercut the Americans. Soon traders and Indians ceased even to visit Fort William.

In 1835 Wyeth took considerable provisions from Fort William to Fort Hall for resale. Returning again to Fort William, he realized that his venture was doomed to fail. In 1836 he gave up and returned to Massachusetts. Later he sailed to London and sold Fort Hall to the Hudson's Bay Company which subsequently occupied it as a Company trading post.

Mt. Hood smokey Dawn

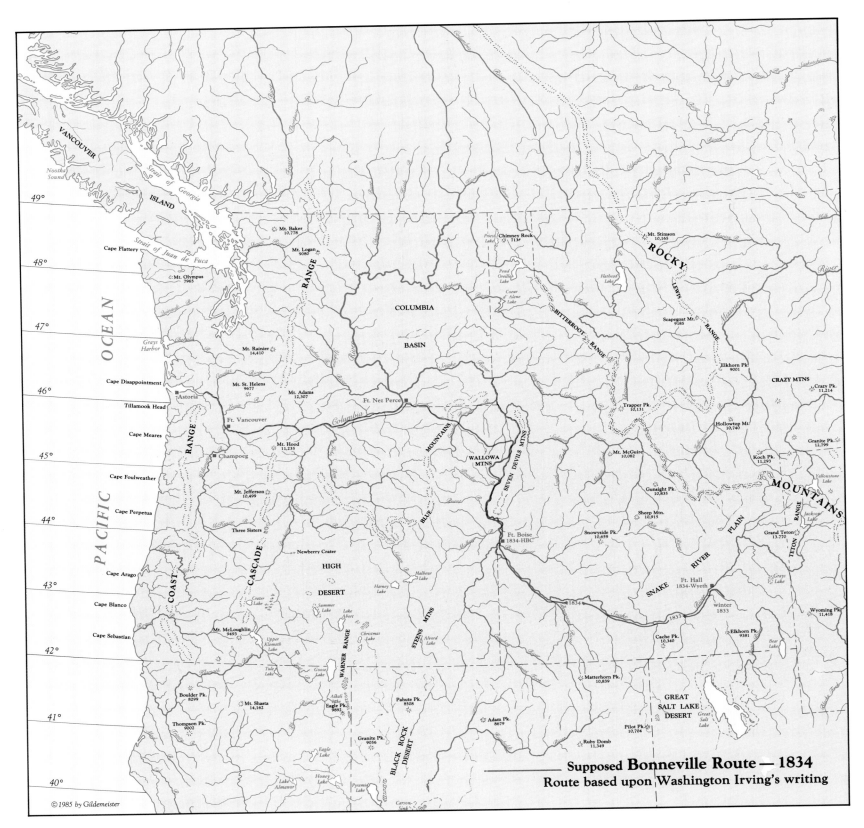

Supposed Bonneville Route — 1834
Route based upon Washington Irving's writing

© 1985 by Gildemeister

Captain Benjamin Bonneville

Benjamin Louis Euladie de Bonneville was born in France. He immigrated to America at an early age and was appointed to the United States Military Academy at West Point. He was graduated in 1819 at age 23, and spent his service on the frontier where he witnessed the comings and goings of the mountain men. From the furs they brought back, Bonneville was led to believe a fortune awaited the enterprising soul with enough nerve to challenge the wilderness.

Bonneville formulated a plan. He arranged a 26-month leave of absence from the Army and, with the financial backing of his family and friends, organized and outfitted a party of 110 men.

Ten days before Nathaniel Wyeth headed west, the only other American expedition of 1832, Bonneville set out from Fort Osage ten miles from Independence, Missouri. The men rode horseback and the ammunition, traps, trading goods and supplies were hauled by twenty wagons pulled by oxen and mules. They followed the route blazed by Astorian Robert Stuart and by trappers up the Platte and Sweetwater rivers and over the Rocky Mountains at South Pass. The wagons, the first taken over the continental divide, were discarded near the rendezvous grounds on Green River.

The expedition explored the headwaters of the Salmon River and spent the winter there. In spring half the men ventured south to explore the Great Salt Lake region, while Bonneville and the others searched the Snake river country for untrapped territory.

The second winter, Bonneville's company camped near the Portneuf River (Idaho). From that base he planned to reconnoiter the Columbia River to acquaint himself with the country and to establish friendly relations with the Indians. In his path lay the desolate Snake river country and the Blue Mountains. He would have to cross in the dead of winter, just as the overland Astorians had.

Bonneville waited while a big storm passed and then he and three other men, riding horses and leading pack mules, turned their backs on winter camp. To save the animals, they were obliged to travel slowly.

January 12, 1834, they reached Powder River and came across a camp of Root Digger Indians. Bonneville described the way they lived: *"…without any further protection from the inclemency of the season than a sort of break-weather, about three feet high, composed of sage, and erected around them in the shape of a half-moon."* He said the Indians were *"destitute of the necessary covering to protect them from the weather; and seemed to be in the most unsophisticated ignorance of any other propriety or advantage in the use of clothing. One old dame had absolutely nothing on her person but a thread round her neck from which was pendent a solitary bead."*

One of the Diggers was employed as guide but he deserted the first day they climbed into higher country. A passing storm brought snow, and late in the afternoon they topped the divide. As low clouds lifted to their benefit they viewed a wonderous sight, the towering snowy peaks of the Wallowa Mountains. They remained a long time contemplating this barrier, then set camp.

In the morning they climbed a neighboring ridge to search out a practical passage but from the vantage it appeared the mountains blocked direct travel, forcing them to skirt out and around. Bonneville decided to cut east, locate the Snake and follow it downstream.

Fog-shrouded Pine Valley & Cornucopia Peak

Two days later they reached the river at the bottom of a deep canyon. They had hoped to travel on the ice but, contrary to their expectations, the river was running free with only an occasional ice bridge and a strip of ice along the shore.

The knife-like edges of incoming gullies and ravines were rounded slightly with a fresh layer of snow and the main canyon dropped steeply until there was only a ribbon of sky above. Nothing existed except the roar of the river and the narrow confines of the canyon. There were giant boulders and perpendicular cliffs, and the four men had to cross back and forth on hazardous ice bridges and at other times lead their horses and mules over imposing rock slides or on game trails that shouldered the wall over a yawning precipice. One saddle horse stumbled over the edge and was swept away by the river.

The small party struggled along the slow and dangerous path downstream to a wall that defied passage. There were two obvious escapes — returning the way they had come or scaling the canyon. Bonneville had a third alternative in mind if they were unsuccessful climbing from the canyon; they would kill their horses and mules, jerky the meat, make hide boats and commit themselves to the rushing current of the Snake River.

The four men led the animals up a perilous zigzag; occasionally a stone would dislodge and roll down the face, picking up momentum, crashing, rebounding. The echoes played across the canyon long after the rock had struck bottom.

It was after dark before they reached a ledge where they could make camp. They slept fitfully. In the morning they went on, and when they finally reached the summit they discovered it was only one ridge in a chain of mountains.

Hells Canyon of the Snake River

Day after day, peak after peak, they struggled. Much of the time they broke trail through the snow for their animals. When the sun came out it melted the snow and made the rocks wet and slippery. In the midst of these uncharted mountains, their supplies gave out. For three dreadful days they were without food. At last they sacrificed one of the mules. For several days they stayed in camp jerking the meat and regaining strength by sucking the marrow of bones.

The journey dragged on, the weary men took turns breaking trail through deep snowdrifts, and just when it seemed they had reached the limits of human endurance they topped the last summit. Far below, stretched like a precious jewel, was the narrow green Imnaha Valley.

Fatigue and hunger were temporarily forgotten as the men made a reckless dash downhill. After the wave of euphoria passed they realized they were still many hours from the bottom. Their legs felt rubbery as they sat to rest, digging heels into the thin dirt to keep from sliding down the incline.

On the valley floor they found a well-worn Indian trail and this encouraging sign lifted the men's spirits. They camped beside the trail and the next day, February 16, after 21 days tangled in the snowy mountains, an Indian on horseback appeared in front of them. He stayed at a distance, apparently studying the four emaciated men and their pathetic animals. When satisfied the strangers could do no harm, he rode to them in a quick gallop. He gave the sign of peace and welcomed them to his village, only a few miles ahead. Then he rode away.

Until now Bonneville had been the strongest of the group, steady as stone, but with deliverance at hand his emotional state unraveled. He sank to the ground. The men implored him to finish the last few miles but he lacked the willpower to move. He slipped into a deep sleep. His companions remained with him and they passed another night.

The next morning Bonneville awoke refreshed and eager to continue. They resumed the measured march a short distance when several Indians galloped up the trail leading fresh horses to bear the white men to camp.

Camp was composed of about twelve families. The white men were welcomed, roots were set out for them and a pipe lighted. The smoke was a welcome luxury since their own supply had been lost in the mountains. These Indians bestowed a whimsical title on Captain Bonneville. Since he was bald he became known by Indian words meaning *Chief With No Hair.*

When Bonneville's party resumed the journey, Indian guides took them from one Nez Perce village to the next. The landscape was magnificent, dominated by the towering mountains behind them.

Bonneville and his companions arrived at Fort Walla Walla the first week of March, 1834. The agent, Pierre Pambrun, was courteous and hospitable. He treated the four Americans as honored guests until Bonneville requested to purchase supplies. The agent's demeanor changed. He said it was the Hudson's Bay Company's policy to do nothing that would encourage competition from rival traders.

Wallowa Mountains

Bonneville, thus rejected, departed Fort Walla Walla traveling slowly, allowing the animals time to recuperate on the new grass. The men subsisted on wild game and the generosity of Indians.

Not knowing another route back to the rendezvous at Portneuf River, they retraced their steps. And when they reached the Imnaha Valley the men stayed in camp while Bonneville, accompanied by two Indian guides, climbed into the mountains. From the vantage of a tall peak Bonneville observed a pass. He sat on a boulder, smoking a pipe and pondering the obstacle — the pass was drifted deep with snow. Swirling wind from an advancing cold front played with the smoke, blew it away. Bonneville thought long and hard. At length, the Indians ventured that horses could not be taken through the pass and suggested the animals be left with them.

Bonneville listened and then told them: *"My friends, I have seen the pass and have listened to your words; you have little hearts. When troubles and dangers lie in your way, you turn your backs. That is not the way with my nation. When great obstacles present, and threaten to keep them back, their hearts swell, and they push forward. They love to conquer difficulties. But enough for the present. Night is coming on; let us return to our camp."*

Bonneville found his men extremely discouraged. They had hiked a short way into the mountains and found deeply drifted snow. Bonneville tried to reassure them, saying he had found a pass but had not yet formulated a plan.

After dark a light drizzle began to fall, freezing as it hit. That was it! Bonneville ordered the men to harness themselves to the sled and pull it through the pass to make a trail. All night they worked. The moon and stars came out and the trail froze solid. They returned to camp in darkness and led the horses along the icy highway. Occasionally a horse would slip out of the track and sink to its neck in the loose snow. The floundering animal would have to be hauled back on the trail with ropes.

Before the sun could weaken the ice, they reached the summit and began the descent. One of the mares took a side step and pitched headlong in the snow. The sun had been shining for some time and the crusted ice was glazed with a fine layer of water. The mare hit this treacherous spot wrong and slid downward with astonishing acceleration. The poor animal squealed and thrashed about trying to check her slide but she fell the faster for her efforts. Two thousand feet she slipped. And then, mixed with the echoes of her last whinny, was the sickening thud of her body dashed against the rock pile at the base.

It was well after dark before the exhausted party reached the lower edges of snow. The following day they reached fresh grass. The difficulties of the mountain crossing were over.

Captain Bonneville and his men reached the Portneuf May 12 to discover the winter encampment had been abandoned. The grounds were searched for a clue to the party's whereabouts, but there was none to be found.

Bonneville and the others were destitute. They traveled south and west hoping to find either food or an Indian tribe which could tell them where the others had gone. They came across a small herd of buffalo and killed two bulls. They camped by the carcasses, keeping the wild animals away and enjoying the jerkied meat.

Again they swung back to Snake River and were surprised to see two white men on the opposite side. Excitedly, Bonneville and the others discharged their rifles as a signal and to their great joy discovered the men were some of their own party. It was learned the main camp was on Blackfoot River, a tributary of the Snake not far above the Portneuf.

The expedition was reunited and two days were given to all the feasting and merriment their means allowed. At the end of this indulgence, Bonneville ordered his motley crew of free trappers, half-breeds, Indians and squaws to break camp for the annual rendezvous at Bear River.

After the conclave Bonneville returned to the Columbia and pushed along the south shore as far as the John Day River. There he was compelled to turn back because of the lateness of the season, the lack of provisions, and the fact that the Indians along the river were under control of the Hudson's Bay Company. They refused even to council with Bonneville for fear trading privileges with the Company would be altered.

The Americans could not exist without provisions. Once more an appeal was made at Fort Walla Walla to purchase supplies and again the request was firmly denied.

Bonneville realized without the support of the Indians his plan to carve out a fur trading pocket in the Northwest was doomed. He turned back east and spent the winter in Bear river valley before reaching the settlements in August 1835.

He discovered he had been dropped from the rolls of the Army for overstaying his leave of absence. An appeal was made, and in time President Jackson honored it in recognition of Bonneville's contribution to opening the door of the Oregon country.

Columbia River Plain

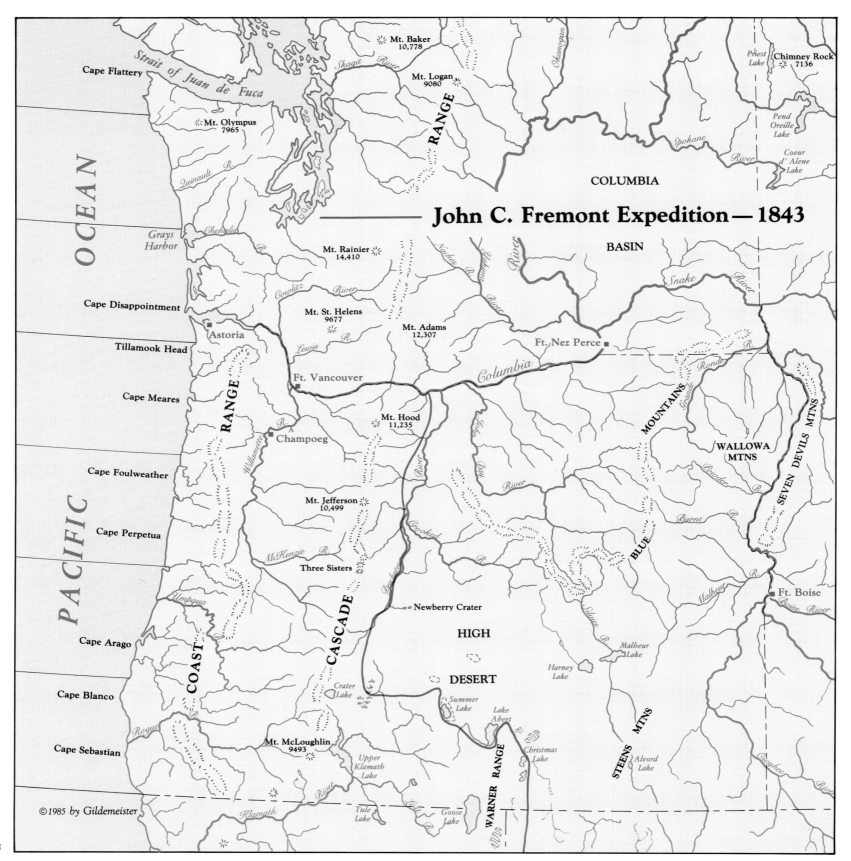

Strait of Juan de Fuca

Cape Flattery

OCEAN

Mt. Olympus
7965

Grays
Harbor

PACIFIC

Cape Disappointment

Astoria

Tillamook Head

Cape Meares

Cape Foulweather

Cape Perpetua

Cape Arago

Cape Blanco

Cape Sebastian

COAST RANGE

Champoeg

Ft. Vancouver

Skagit River

Mt. Baker
10,778

Mt. Logan
9080

RANGE

Mt. Rainier
14,410

Mt. St. Helens
9677

Mt. Adams
12,307

Cowlitz River

Lewis R.

Columbia

Mt. Hood
11,235

CASCADE RANGE

Mt. Jefferson
10,499

McKenzie R.

Three Sisters

Newberry Crater

Crater Lake

Mt. McLoughlin
9493

Upper Klamath Lake

Klamath River

Tule Lake

Quinault R.

Chehalis R.

Willamette R.

Umpqua R.

Rogue R.

John C. Fremont Expedition — 1843

COLUMBIA

BASIN

Shanogan

Priest Lake

Chimney Rock
7136

Pend Oreille Lake

Spokane River

Coeur d' Alene Lake

Snake River

Ft. Nez Perce

MOUNTAINS

Grande Ronde R.

BLUE

WALLOWA MTNS

SEVEN DEVILS MTNS

Powder R.

Burnt R.

Malheur R.

Ft. Boise

Boise River

HIGH

DESERT

Crooked River

Deschutes River

Silvies R.

Malheur Lake

Harney Lake

Summer Lake

Lake Abert

Christmas Lake

Goose Lake

WARNER RANGE

STEENS MTNS

Alvord Lake

Owyhee River

© 1985 by Gildemeister

John Charles Fremont

John Charles Fremont was born in Georgia in 1813. He was appointed second lieutenant in the topographical engineers of the United States Army at age 25, but not until after eloping with Missouri Senator Thomas Benton's daughter Jessie on October 19, 1841, did he begin his quick rise in military leadership. With the senator's assistance, Fremont was appointed in early 1843 to lead a survey expedition of the Oregon country.

As the survey expedition was organized, fellow officers who had not advanced as quickly protested to Washington and succeeded in having the expedition cancelled. They charged that Fremont was taking a howitzer along and his mission could not be one of surveying if he were toting a cannon. A message was dispatched from Washington but Jessie was informed of the plot and sent her husband a note advising him to start out at once and to keep going. Fremont, upon receiving Jessie's note, promptly ordered the expedition to pull out and the dispatch never caught up with them.

On October 25, 1843, Fremont arrived at Fort Walla Walla. They continued down the Columbia to the Deschutes River and turned south following a well-defined Indian trail. The guides for this portion of the journey included Kit Carson, the renowned frontiersman, and Billy Chinook, a Warm Springs Indian.

Fremont made note on November 26, 1843: *"The morning was cloudy and misty, and but a few stars visible. During the night water froze in the tents, and at sunrise the thermometer was at 20°....Snow lies everywhere here on the ground, and we had a slight fall during the morning; but toward noon the gray sky yielded to a bright sun....In anticipation of coming hardship, and to spare our horses, there was much walking done to-day...."*

November 27: "*A fine view of Mount Hood this morning; a rose-colored mass of snow. The sky is clear, and the air cold; the trees and bushes glittering white, and the rapid stream filled with floating ice....The country is now far more interesting to a traveller than the route along the Snake and Columbia Rivers. To our right we had always the mountains, from the midst of whose dark pine forests the isolated snowy peaks were looking out like giants. They served us for grand beacons to show the rate at which we advanced in our journey. Mount Hood was already becoming an old acquaintance, and when we ascended the prairie, we obtained a bearing to Mount Jefferson.*

"*The Indian superstition has peopled these lofty peaks with evil spirits, and they have never yet known the tread of a human foot. Sternly drawn against the sky, they look so high and steep, so snowy and rocky, that it would appear almost impossible to climb them; but still a trail would have its attractions for the adventurous traveler.*"

November 30: "*...the country is abundantly watered with large streams which pour down from the neighboring range. These streams are characterized by the narrow and chasm-like valleys in which they run, generally sunk a thousand feet below the plain. At the verge of this plain they frequently commence in vertical precipices of basaltic rock, and which leave only casual places at which they can be entered by horses. The road across the country, which would otherwise be very good, is rendered impracticable for wagons by these streams....the gun-carriage was unlimbered, and separately descended by hand. Continuing a few miles up the left bank of the river, we encamped early in an open bottom among the pines, a short distance below a lodge of Indians. Here, along the river, the bluffs present escarpments seven or eight hundred feet in height, containing strata of a very fine porcelain clay, overlaid, at the height of about five hundred feet, by a massive stratum of compact basalt one hundred feet in thickness, which again is succeeded above by other strata of volcanic rocks....*"

December 2: "*In the first rays of the sun the mountain peaks this morning presented a beautiful appearance, the snow being entirely covered with a hue of rosy gold....*"

Mt. Hood

Ponderosa Pine on the Dechutes Plain

December 5: *"To-day the country was all pine forest, and beautiful weather made our journey delightful. I was too warm at noon for winter clothes; and the snow, which lays everywhere in patches through the forest, was melting rapidly.*

"After a few hours' ride we came upon a fine stream in the midst of the forest, which proved to be the principal branch of Fall River [Deschutes River]. *It was occasionally two hundred feet wide — sometimes narrowed to fifty feet; the waters very clear, and frequently deep. We ascended along the river which sometimes presented sheets of foaming cascades....The timber was uniformly large; some of the pines measuring twenty-two feet in circumference at the ground, and twelve to thirteen feet at six feet above.*

"In all our journeying we had never travelled through a country where the rivers were so abounding in falls, and the name of this stream is singularly characteristic. At every place we come in the neighborhood of the river is heard the roaring of falls...."

December 8: *"To-day we crossed the last branch of the Fall River, issuing, like all the others we had crossed, in a southwesterly direction from the mountains. Our direction was a little east of south, the trail leading constantly through pine forests....These pines are remarkable for the red color of the boles; and among them occurs a species* [sugar pine], *of which the Indians had informed me when leaving the Dalles. The unusual size of the cone, sixteen or eighteen inches long, had attracted their attention; and they pointed it out to me among the curiosities of the country. They are more remarkable for their large diameter than their height, which usually averages only about one hundred and twenty feet...."*

Klamath Marsh

December 10: *"The country began to improve; and about eleven o'clock we reached a spring of cold water on the edge of a savannah, or grassy meadow, which our guides informed us was an arm of the Tlamath Lake; and a few miles further we entered upon an extensive meadow, or lake of grass, surrounded by timbered mountains. This was the Tlamath Lake [actually Klamath Marsh]. It was a picturesque and beautiful spot, and rendered more attractive to us by the abundant and excellent grass, which our animals, after traveling through pine forests, so much needed; but the broad sheet of the water which constitutes a lake was not to be seen. Overlooking it, immediately west, were several snowy knobs, belonging to what we have considered a branch of the Cascade range. A low point covered with pines made out into the lake, which afforded us a good place for an encampment and for the security of our horses, which were guarded in view on the open meadow.*

"The character of courage and hostility attributed to the Indians of this quarter induced more than usual precaution; and, seeing smokes rising from the middle of the lake and along the opposite shores, I directed the howitzer to be fired. It was the first time our guides had seen it discharged; and the bursting of the shell at a distance, which was something like the second fire of the gun, amazed and bewildered them with delight. It inspired them with triumphant feelings; but on the camps at a distance the effect was different, for the smokes in the lake and on the shore immediately disappeared...."

December 13: *"The night has been cold; the peaks around the lake gleam out brightly in the morning sun, and the thermometer is at zero. We continued up the hollow formed by a small affluent to the lake, and immediately entered an open pine forest on the mountain. The way here was sometimes obstructed by fallen trees, and the snow was four to twelve inches deep. The mules at the gun pulled heavily, and walking was a little laborious.*

"In the midst of the wood we heard the sound of galloping horses, and were agreeably surprised by the unexpected arrival of our Tlamath chief with several Indians. He seemed to have found his conduct inhospitable in letting the strangers depart without a guide through the snow, and had come, with a few others, to pilot us a day or two on the way...."

December 16: "*We travelled this morning through snow about three feet deep, which, being crusted, very much cut the feet of our animals. The mountain still gradually rose; we crossed several spring heads covered with quaking asp, otherwise it was all pine forest. The air was dark with falling snow, which everywhere weighed down the trees. The depth of the forest were profoundly still; and below, we scarce felt a breath of the wind which whirled the snow through their branches.*

"*...Toward noon the forest looked clear ahead, appearing suddenly to terminate; and beyond a certain point we could see no trees. Riding rapidly ahead to this spot, we found ourselves on the verge of a vertical and rocky wall of the mountain.*

"*At our feet — more than a thousand feet below — we looked into a green prairie country, in which a beautiful lake, some twenty miles in length, was spread along the foot of the mountains, its shores bordered with green grass. Just then the sun broke out among the clouds, and illuminated the country below, while around us the storm raged fiercely. Not a particle of ice was to be seen on the lake, or snow on its borders, and all was like summer or spring. The glow of the sun in the valley below brightened up our hearts with sudden pleasure; and we made the woods ring with the joyful shouts to those behind; and gradually, as each came up, he stopped to enjoy the unexpected scene. Shivering on snow three feet deep, and stiffening in a cold north wind, we exclaimed at once that the names of Summer Lake and Winter Ridge should be applied to these two proximate places of such sudden and violent contrast. When we had sufficiently admired the scene below, we began to think about descending, which here was impossible, and we turned toward the north, travelling always along the rocky wall. We continued on for four or five miles, making ineffectual attempts at several places; and at length succeeded in getting down at one which was extremely difficult of descent. Night had closed in before the foremost reached the bottom, and it was dark before we all found ourselves together in the valley. There were three or four half-dead dry cedar-trees on the shore, and those who first arrived kindled bright fires to light on the others.*

Summer Lake-Winter Ridge

Abert Lake

"One of the mules rolled over and over two or three hundred feet into a ravine, but recovered himself, without any other injury than to his pack; and the howitzer was left mid-way the mountain until morning...."

December 20: "...Throughout this region the face of the country is characterized by precipices of black volcanic rock, generally enclosing the valleys of stream, and frequently terminating the hills.

"Often in the course of our journey we would be tempted to continue our road up the gentle ascent of a sloping hill, which, at the summit, would terminate abruptly in a black precipice. Spread out over a length of twenty miles, the lake, when we first came in view, presented a handsome sheet of water; and I gave to it the name of Lake Abert, in honor of the chief of the corps to which I belonged.

"...We were following an Indian trail which led along the steep rocky precipice; a black ridge along the western shore holding out no prospect whatever. The white efflorescences which lined the shore like a bank of snow, and the disagreeable odor which filled the air as soon as we came near, informed us too plainly that the water belonged to one of those fetid salt lakes which are common in this region.

"We continued until late in the evening to work along the rocky shore, but, as often afterward, the dry inhospitable rock deceived us; and, halting on the lake, we kindled up fires to guide those who were straggling along behind. We tried the water, but it was impossible to drink it, and most of the people to-night lay down without eating; but some of us, who had always a great reluctance to close the day without supper, dug holes along the shore, and obtained water, which, being filtered, was sufficiently palatable to be used, but still retained much of its nauseating taste...."

December 22: "To-day we left this forbidding lake. Impassable rocky ridges barred our progress to the eastward, and I accordingly bore off toward the south, over an extensive sage plain...."

December 25: "We were roused on Christmas morning, by a discharge from the small arms and howitzer, with which our people saluted the day; and the name (Christmas Lake) of which we bestowed on the lake [now known as Hart Lake]. It was the first time, perhaps, in this remote and desolate region, in which it had been so commemorated.

"Always, on days of religious or national commemoration, our voyageurs expect some unusual allowance; and, having nothing else, I gave them each a little brandy, which was carefully guarded as one of the most useful articles a traveller can carry, with some coffee and sugar, which here, where every eatable was a luxury, we sufficient to make them a feast...."

December 31: "...Here we concluded the year 1843, and our new year's eve was rather a gloomy one. The result of our journey began to be very uncertain; the country was singularly unfavorable to travel; the grasses being frequently of a very unwholesome character, and the hoofs of our animals were so worn and cut by the rocks, that many of them were lame, and could scarcely be got along."

Fremont's expedition passed over the 42nd parallel into the Mexican province of Alta California. They crossed the Sierra Nevada during a winter storm and arrived at Sutter's fort on the Sacramento River March 6, 1844. During their ordeal they had subsisted on the flesh of horses, mules and dogs.

On his return to Washington, Fremont was promoted to captain. The following year he was sent again across the plains, this time to investigate the country west of Salt Lake. After completing the survey he swung north and entered Oregon in the Klamath Lake region with the intention of locating a pass to the Willamette Valley. According to his journal: "My plan when I started on my journey into this region were to connect my present survey of the intervening country with my camp on the savannah, where I had met the Tlamaths in that December; and I wished to penetrate among the mountains of the Cascade range [to the Willamette Valley]. As I have said, except for the few trappers who had searched the streams leading to the ocean, for beaver, I felt sure that these mountains were absolutely unknown. No one had penetrated their recesses to know what they contained, and no one had climbed to their summits; and there remained the great attraction of mystery in going into unknown places — the unknown lands of which I had dreamed when I began this life of frontier travel...."

"How fate pursues a man! Thinking and ruminating over these things, I was standing alone by my camp-fire, enjoying its warmth, for the night air of early spring is chill under the shadows of the high mountains. Suddenly my ear caught the faint sound of horses' feet, and while I was watching and listening as the sounds, so strange hereabout, came nearer, there emerged from the darkness — into the circle of the firelight — two horsemen, riding slowly as though horse and man were fatigued by long travel. In the foremost I recognized the familiar face of Neal, with a companion whom I also knew. They had ridden nearly a hundred miles in the last two days, having been sent foreward by a United States officer who was on my trail with dispatches for me; but Neal doubted if he could get through. After their horses had been turned into the band and they were seated by my fire, refreshing themselves with good coffee while more solid food was being prepared, Neal told me his story. The officer who was trying to overtake me was named Gillespie. He had been sent by the Government and had letters for delivery to me...."

"When the excitement of the evening was over I lay down, speculating far into the night on what could be the urgency of the message which had brought an officer of the Government to search so far after me into these mountains. At early dawn we took the backward trail....In the afternoon, having made about forty-five miles, we reached the spot where the forest made an opening to the lake, and where I intended to wait. This was a glade, or natural meadow, shut in by the forest, with a small stream and good grass, where I had already encamped. I knew that this was the first water to which my trail would bring the messenger, and that I was sure to meet him here if no harm befell him on the way. The sun was about going down when he was seen issuing from the wood, accompanied by three men.

"He proved to be an officer of the navy, Lieutenant Archibald Gillespie of the Marine Corps. We greeted him warmly. All were glad to see him, white and Indians. It was long since any news had reached us....It was now eleven months since any tidings had reached me.

"...Through him I now become acquainted with the actual state of affairs and the purposes of the Government. The information through Gillespie had absolved me from my duty as an explorer, and I was left to my duty as an officer of the American Army with the further authoritative knowledge that the Government intended to take California. I was warned by my Government of the new danger against which I was bound to defend myself; and it had been made known to me now on the authority of the Secretary of the Navy that to obtain possession of California was the chief object of the President.

"I had about thought out the situation when I was startled by the sudden movement among the animals. Lieutenant Gillespie had told me that there were no Indians on his trail, and I knew there were none on mine. This night was one of two (during nearly 20,000 miles of wilderness exploration) when I failed to put men on guard in an Indian country — this night and one spent on an island in the Great Salt Lake. The animals were near the shore of the lake, barely a hundred yards away. Drawing a revolver I went down amoung them. A mule is a good sentinel, and when he quits eating and stands with his ears stuck straight out taking notice, it is best to see what is the matter. The mules knew that Indians were around, but nothing seemed stirring, and my presence quieting the animals I returned to the fire and my letters.

"I saw the way opening clear before me. War with Mexico was inevitable; and a grand opportunity now presented itself to realize in their fullest extent the far-sighted views of Senator Benton, and make the Pacific Ocean the western boundary of the United States....

"My mind having settled into this conclusion, I went to my blankets under a cedar. The camp was divided into three fires, and near each one, but well out of the light, were sleeping the men belonging to it. Close up along the margin of the wood which shut us in on three sides were some low cedars, the ends of their boughs reaching nearly to the ground. Under these we made our bed.

"One always likes to have his head sheltered, and a rifle with a ramrod or a branch or bush with a blanket thrown over it answers very well where there is nothing better. I had barely fallen to sleep when I was awakened by the sound of Carson's voice, calling to Basil to know 'what the matter was over there?' No reply came, and immediately the camp was roused by the cry from Kit and Owens, who were lying together — 'Indians.' Basil and the half-breed, Denny, had been killed. It was the sound of the axe being driven into Basil's head that had awakened Carson. The half-breed had been killed with arrows, and his groans had replied to Carson's call, and told him what the matter was. No man with an Indian experience, jumps squarely to his feet in a night attack but in an instant every man was at himself. The Delawares who lay near their fire on that side sprung to cover, rifle in hand, at the sound of the axe. We ran to their aid, Carson and I, Godey, Stepp, and Owens, just as the Tlamaths charged into the open ground. The fires were smouldering, but gave light enough to show Delaware Crane jumping like a brave as he was from side to side in Indian fashion, and defending himself with the butt of his gun. By some mischance his rifle was not loaded when he lay down. All this was quick work. The moment's silence which followed Carson's shout was broken by our rifles. The Tlamath chief, who was at the head of his men, fell in front of Crane, who was just down with five arrows in his body — three in his breast. The Tlamaths, checked in their onset and disconcerted by the fall of their chief, jumped back into the shadow of the wood. We threw a blanket over Crane and hung blankets to the cedar boughs and bushes near by, behind my camp-fire, for a defense against the arrows. The Indians did not dare to put themselves again in the open, but continued to pour in their arrows. They made no attempt on our animals, which had been driven up by Owens to be under fire of the camp, but made frequent attempts to get the body of their chief. We were determined they should not have it, and every movement on their part brought a rifle-shot; a dozen rifles in such hands at short range made the undertaking too hazardous for them to persist in it....

"All night we lay behind our blanket defenses, with our rifles cocked in our hands, expecting momentarily another attack, until the morning light enabled us to see the Indians had disappeared. By their tracks we found that fifteen or twenty Tlamaths had attacked us. It was a sorrowful sight that met our eyes in the gray of the morning. Three of our men had been killed: Basil, Crane, and the half-breed Denny, and another Delaware had been wounded....The chief who had been killed was recognized to be the same Indian who had given Lieutenant Gillespie a salmon....Hung to his wrist was an English half-axe. Carson seized this and knocked his head to pieces with it, and one of the Delawares, Sagundai, scalped him. He was left where he fell. In his quiver were forty arrows; as Carson said 'the most beautiful and warlike arrows he had ever seen.' We saw more of them afterward. These arrows were all headed with a lancet-like piece of iron or steel — probably obtained from the Hudson Bay Company's traders on the Umpqua — and were poisoned for about six inches. They could be driven that depth into a pine tree.

"This event cast an angry gloom over the little camp. For the moment I threw all other considerations aside and determined to square accounts with these people before I left them....

"...The Delawares were filled with grief and rage by the death of Crane and went into mourning, blackening their faces. They were soothed somewhat when I told them that they should have an opportunity to get rid of their mourning and carry home scalps enough to satisfy the friends of Crane and the Delaware nation. With blackened faces, set and angry, they sat around brooding and waiting for revenge.

"...Continuing our route along the lake we passed around the extreme northwestern bay and after a hard day's march encamped in the midst of the woods....We were not very far from the principal village at the inlet which the Indians whom I had met when I first reached the lake had described to me; and the arms being all carefully examined and packs made secure, we started for it. When within a few miles I sent Carson and Owens ahead with ten men, directing them to reconnoiter the position of the Indians, but if possible to avoid engaging them until we could come up. But, as we neared the mouth of the river [Williamson River], the firing began....The stream was about sixty yards wide and a rapid just above the mouth made it fordable. Without drawing rein we plunged in and crossed to the farther side and joined our men, who were pressed by a large body of Indians. They had abandoned their village and were scattered through a field of sage-brush, in front of the woods. But this time the night was not on their side and the attack was with us. Their arrows were good at close quarters, but the range of the rifle was better. The firing was too severe for them to stand it in open ground and they were driven back into the pine woods with a loss of fourteen killed. They had intended to make a hard fight. Behind the sage-brushes where they had taken their stand every Indian had spread his arrows on the ground in fan-like shape, so they would be ready to his hand. But when our close fire drove them from the brush they were compelled to move so quickly that many did not have time to gather up their arrows and they lay on the ground, the bright, menacing points turned toward us. Quantities of fish were drying, spread on scaffolds, or hung up on frames. The huts, which were made of tall rushes and willow, like those on the savannah above, were set on fire, and the fish and scaffolds were all destroyed.

"About a mile from the village I made my camp...in the midst of woods, where were oaks intermingled with pines, and built a strong corral. Meantime I kept out scouts on every side and horses were kept saddled. In the afternoon Indians were reported advancing through the timber; and taking with me Carson, Sagundai, Swonok, Stepp, and Archambeau, I rode out to see what they were intending. Sacramento [Fremont's saddle horse] knew how to jump and liked it. Going through the wood at a hand-gallop we came upon an oak tree which had been blown down; its summit covered quite a space, and being crowded by the others so that I was brought squarely in front of it, I let Sacramento go and he cleared the whole green mass in a beautiful leap....

"In the heart of the wood we came suddenly upon an Indian scout. He was drawing his arrow to the head as we came upon him, and Carson attempted to fire, but his rifle snapped, and as he swerved away the Indian was about to let his arrow go into him; I fired, and in my haste to save Carson, failed to kill the Indian, but Sacramento, as I have said, was not afraid of anything, and I jumped him directly upon the Indian and threw him to the ground. His arrow went wild. Sagundai was right behind me, and as I passed over the Indian he threw himself from his horse and killed him with a blow on the head from his war-club. It was the work of a moment, but it was a narrow chance for Carson. The poisoned arrow would have gone through his body.

"Giving Sacramento into the care of Jacob, I went into the lodge and laid down on my blankets to rest from the excitement of which the day had been so full. I had now kept the promise I made to myself and had punished these people well for their treachery; and now I turn my thoughts to the work which they had delayed. I was lost in conjectures over this new field when Gillespie came in, all roused into emotion. 'By Heaven, this is rough work,' he exclaimed. 'I'll take care to let them know in Washington about it.' 'Heaven don't come in for much about here, just now,' I said; 'and as for Washington, it will be long enough before we see it again; time enough to forget about this.'"

Fremont passed from the Klamath country, his accounts preserved in the annals of Oregon history. He traveled south and became involved in the struggle for possession of California. All together he made five western explorations between 1842 and 1854. Later he entered national politics where he stood as the Republican Party's first presidential candidate (1856) but was defeated by James Buchanan.

Klamath Lake & Mt. McLoughlin

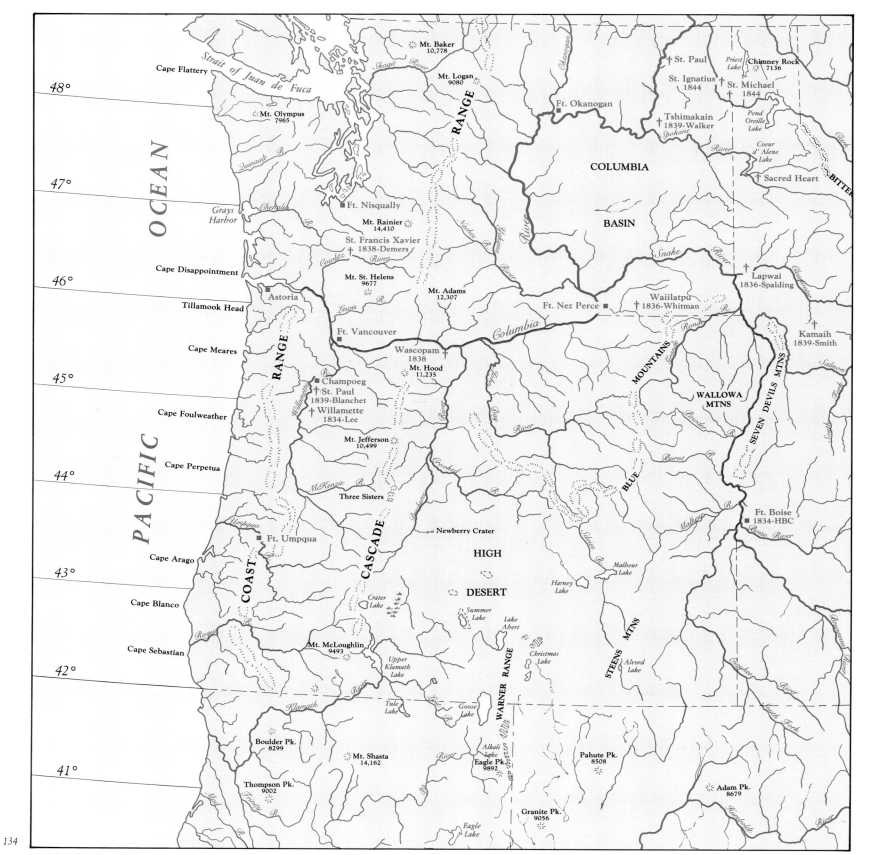

48°
47°
46°
45°
44°
43°
42°
41°

OCEAN
PACIFIC

Strait of Juan de Fuca
Cape Flattery
Mt. Olympus 7965
Grays Harbor
Cape Disappointment
Tillamook Head
Cape Meares
Cape Foulweather
Cape Perpetua
Cape Arago
Cape Blanco
Cape Sebastian

Skagit River
Mt. Baker 10,778
Mt. Logan 9080
Ft. Okanogan
Ft. Nisqually
Mt. Rainier 14,410
St. Francis Xavier 1838-Demers
Mt. St. Helens 9677
Mt. Adams 12,307
Astoria
Ft. Vancouver
Columbia
Wascopam 1838
Mt. Hood 11,235
Champoeg
†St. Paul 1839-Blanchet
†Willamette 1834-Lee
Mt. Jefferson 10,499
McKenzie R.
Three Sisters
Ft. Umpqua
Newberry Crater
Crater Lake
HIGH
DESERT
Summer Lake
Lake Abert
Christmas Lake
Mt. McLoughlin 9493
Upper Klamath Lake
Tule Lake
Goose Lake
Alkali Lake
Boulder Pk. 8299
Mt. Shasta 14,162
Eagle Pk. 9892
Thompson Pk. 9002
Eagle Lake
Granite Pk. 9056

COLUMBIA
BASIN
RANGE
COAST RANGE
CASCADE RANGE
WARNER RANGE

† St. Paul
Priest Lake
Chimney Rock 7136
St. Ignatius 1844
St. Michael 1844
Tshimakain 1839-Walker
Pend Oreille Lake
Coeur d' Alene Lake
† Sacred Heart
BITTER
Spokane River
Snake River
Lapwai 1836-Spalding
Waiilatpu † 1836-Whitman
Ft. Nez Perce
Kamaih 1839-Smith
MOUNTAINS
WALLOWA MTNS
BLUE
SEVEN DEVILS MTNS
Ft. Boise 1834-HBC
Boise River
STEENS MTNS
Malheur Lake
Harney Lake
Alvord Lake
Pahute Pk. 8508
Adam Pk. 8679

The Missionary Movement

The fall of 1831 four Indians appeared in St. Louis, two Flatheads and two Nez Perce. They had come to speak with the man they called *Great Father*, William Clark, who had visited them more than a quarter century before as one of the leaders of the Lewis and Clark expedition. They came, they said, on behalf of all Indians asking for the *Great Father* to share the white man's God.

The plight of these suppliants was first published in French by the Catholic bishop of St. Louis, the Rt. Rev. Joseph Rosati: *"Some three months ago four Indians, who live at the other side of the Rocky Mountains, near the Columbia River, arrived in St. Louis. After visiting General Clark, who, in his celebrated travels, had seen the nation to which they belonged, and had been well received by them, they came to see our church, and appeared to be exceedingly pleased with it. Unfortunately there was no one who understood their language. Sometime afterward two of them fell dangerously ill. I was then absent from St. Louis. Two of our priests visited them, and the poor Indians seemed delighted with their visit. They made sign of the cross, and other signs which appear to have some relation to baptism. The sacrament was administered to them; they gave expression of their satisfaction. A little cross was presented to them; they took it with eagerness, kissed it repeatedly, and it could be taken from them only after their death. It was truly distressing that they could not be spoken to. Their remains were carried to the church for the funeral, which was conducted with all the Catholic ceremonies. The other two attended and acted with great propriety. They have returned to their country."*

The register of burials of the cathedral in St. Louis lists the Indians with their baptismal names; Narcisse was buried October 31, 1831, and Paul was buried November 17, 1831.

George Catlin, who spent eight years living among and painting the Indians of the Northwest, was a passenger on the steamboat when the two survivors of the Indian delegation started up the Missouri toward their home. In a letter Catlin wrote that the Indians had come *"to inquire for the truth of a representation which they said some white men had made amongst them 'that our religion was better than theirs, and that they would all be lost if they did not embrace it.' The old and venerable men of this party died in St. Louis, and I travelled two thousand miles companion of these two young fellows toward their own country, and became much pleased with their manners and dispositions. The last mentioned of the two died near the mouth of the Yellowstone River on his way home, with disease which he had contracted in the civilized district, and the other one I have since learned arrived safely amongst his friends, conveying to them the melancholy intelligence of the deaths of all the rest of his party; but assurances at the same time from Gen. Clark and many reverend gentlemen, that the report which they had heard was well founded; and that missionaries, good and religious men, would soon come amongst them to teach this religion so they could all understand and have the benefits of it...."*

The American public did not become aware of the Indians' hunger for religion until March 1, 1833, when the leading journal of the Methodist church, the **Christian Advocate**, published a letter by frontiersman William Walker:

"...Curiosity prompted me to step into the adjoining room [General William Clark's home] to see them [Flathead Indians], having never seen any, but often heard of them. I was struck with their appearance. They differ in appearance from any of Indians I have ever seen; small in size, delicately formed, small limbs, and the most exact symmetry throughout, except the head. I had always supposed from their being called 'Flatheads', that the head was actually flat on top. But this is not the case....General Clark related to me their mission, and, my dear friend, it is impossible for me to describe to you my feelings while listening to his narrative. I will here relate it as briefly as I can. It appeared that some white man had penetrated into their country, and had happened to be a spectator at one of their religious meetings, which they scrupulously perform at stated periods. He informed them that their mode of worshiping the Supreme Being was radically wrong, and instead of being acceptable and pleasing was displeasing to Him. He also informed them that the white people, away toward the rising sun, had been put in possession of the true mode of worshiping the Great Spirit....Upon receiving this information they held a national council to take this subject into consideration....They accordingly deputed four of their chiefs to proceed to St. Louis to see their Great Father, General Clark, to inquire of him, having no doubt but he would tell them the whole truth about it.

"They arrived in St. Louis and presented themselves to General Clark. The latter was somewhat puzzled, being sensible of the responsibility that rested upon him. He, however proceeded, by informing them that what they had been told by the white men in their own country was true. He then went into a succinct history of man, from the creation down to the advent of the Savior, explained to them all the moral precepts of the Bible, expounded to them the decalogue, informed them of the advent of the Savior. His life, precepts, His death, resurrection and ascension, and the relation He stands to man as mediator, the judgment, that He will judge the world...."

It was this story of Walker's, appealing strongly to Christian sentiment, that awakened the country to the Indians' need to have God brought to the wilderness. The response was immediate. The Board of Missions of the Methodist Episcopal Church appropriated $3,000 to outfit a mission to the Indians. One of the first to volunteer was the Reverend Jason Lee. He was appointed superintendent of the first mission west of the Rockies.

The Reverend Jason Lee

When Jason Lee volunteered to lead the missionary expedition to the Columbia river region he was preaching near his birthplace in Stanstead, Ontario, Canada. He was tall, strong and possessed a zealous desire to spread the word of his faith.

Lee was officially commissioned July 17, 1833, and immediately began a tour of the eastern states speaking at churches and asking for parishioners' support. In Boston he met Nathaniel Wyeth, recently returned from his first expedition and making plans for the second. It was arranged that the expedition ship, the *May Dacre*, would carry supplies to start a mission in the Oregon country; Lee and the other missionaries would travel overland with Wyeth's company.

On April 28, 1834, a peculiar blend of fur trappers and missionaries departed Fort Independence. Two months later they reached the rendezvous of Rocky Mountain trappers on Hams Fork. A month after that they made Snake River. While waiting for Wyeth to build Fort Hall, Jason Lee delivered the first sermon west of the Rocky Mountains. His congregation of missionaries, fur traders and Indians sat on the sand.

Later the Indians presented the missionaries with two fine, white horses, prompting Lee to write in his journal July 30, 1834: *"Surely, the hand of Providence must be in it, for they presented them because we are missionaries, and at a time when two of our horses were nearly worn out. This, if I mistake not, augurs well for our ultimate success among these generous red men."*

The Wyeth men remained to establish Fort Hall as a trading post, but the missionaries were impatient to reach the Columbia. They employed Captain William Stewart, a Scotch sportsman who was on a hunting expedition in the far West, and Thomas McKay, a Hudson's Bay man in the area, to guide them to the river. At last, late in September, they arrived at Fort Vancouver. After 152 nights of sleeping under the stars they slept indoors on beds.

Lee planned to pick up the supplies sent with the *May Dacre* and return to the Flathead nation to establish a mission. Dr. John McLoughlin advised Lee: *"…it was too dangerous for him to establish a mission [among the Flathead]; that to do good to the Indians they must establish themselves where they could collect them around them; teach them first to cultivate the ground, and live more comfortably that they do by hunting, and, as they do this, teach them religion; that the Willamette [Valley] afforded them a fine field, and that they ought to go there…."*

Services were held at Fort Vancouver the first Sunday after the missionaries arrived and $130 was contributed toward establishing a mission nearby. Dr. McLoughlin offered a Company boat and Company guides and oarsmen if Lee would take a look at the Willamette Valley.

Jason Lee and his nephew Daniel Lee examined the Willamette Valley and found it blessed with timber, a favorable climate, fertile soil and adequate water. Sixty miles from the mouth of the Willamette River (a few miles north of today's Salem) tents were pitched on the east bank near a melon patch belonging to Joseph Gervais. Gervais was a French-Canadian and former member of the Astor overland expedition who chose to stay and farm after the company was sold. Here, on October 6, 1834, the first regular missionary station was established. Work began on a 32-foot by 18-foot log building. Lee used his pocket knife to whittle sashes for the windows and carved a pair of wooden hinges to hang the door.

School was held in this building but of the 14 Indian children attending the first year, five died and five ran away. Of the remaining four, two died in the second year. White man's diseases, smallpox, diphtheria, malaria, measles and fevers, devastated the native population. Families, whole villages and even tribes were totally annihilated.

Jason Lee wrote a long letter to a superior on March 15, 1836. He was discouraged. Caring for the sick and farming for subsistence took all his time and he saw no more evidence of success than that one native had been converted to Christianity. He requested more missionaries.

Reinforcements came from the east coast by ship. Three were unmarried women. One of them, Anna Maria Pittman, had been given to understand by the Missionary Society that marriage to Mr. Lee would be a possibility and Lee had been advised that Miss Pittman would be a suitable wife. Within a few months of their meeting they were married.

The following spring, to assure his mission's success, Lee reluctantly decided to leave his bride and return overland to the East to appeal for additional money and lay participation, particularly doctors, farmers and blacksmiths.

Lee was accompanied by Philip Edwards, a teacher at the mission, and two Indians and three half-breed boys. Together they made an extensive tour of the States. The boys, delivering short, well-practiced speeches, never failed to attract attention. Lee told stories of the Oregon country, encouraged settlement and government by Americans and asked for volunteers and money.

During that winter, $40,000 was raised for the Oregon mission but equally important were the fifty volunteers, including 16 children, who became known as the *Great Reinforcement*. They arrived in Oregon by ship on June 1, 1840, and on the 13th a general meeting was held in which Lee assigned members to three missions he planned to establish — Nisqually on Puget Sound, Clatsop on the lower Columbia and another in the Umpqua region. The Umpqua mission was soon found impractical because, in the words of the Reverend H.K. Hines: *"The Indians were few and scattered, degraded and cruel. They were evidently dying away* [from disease], *and as a people without hope and without remedy. Though a mission might save individuals, as a people they could not be saved....They were darkly, terribly, certainly doomed."*

The Mission Board, separated from the Willamette Valley by the width of a continent, judged success by the number of Indians converted to Christianity. The low number of converts and the vast sum of money dedicated to the missionary work led the board, in July 1843, to remove Jason Lee as superintendent of the Oregon missions and replace him with the Reverend George Gary.

Dr. Marcus Whitman and Associates

During the 1830s, numerous missionaries were sent to the Oregon country. Roman Catholics, called *black gowns* by the Indians, included the Reverend Fathers Francis Norbert Blanchet, Modeste Demers and P.J. DeSmet. Protestant clergymen were also called to the Indian country, as well as missionaries sent by congregational associations. But the most famous of all were Dr. Marcus Whitman and his associates.

The effort of Dr. Whitman was sponsored by the American Board of Commissioners for Foreign Missions, an organization maintained by the Presbyterian, Congregationalist and Dutch Reformed churches. In 1835 Dr. Whitman organized a missionary expedition outfitted with material for a blacksmith shop, along with farm implements, seeds and clothing.

It was the view of the American Board that married missionaries were preferable. This led Dr. Whitman to take as his wife Narcissa Prentiss of New York. She was a blue-eyed, blonde lady of commanding appearance, big-boned and full-figured, strong-willed and not given to swings in emotion. At the farewell meeting in the little church she had so long attended, Narcissa was the only one able to conclude the hymn. One by one the other voices broke into sobs, but hers was clear and unwavering:

> *Yes, my native land, I love thee,*
> *All the scenes I love them well;*
> *Friends, connections, happy country,*
> *Can I bid you all farewell?*

Thirty-four-year-old Dr. Whitman was designated by the board to lead the missionary party composed of him and his wife, the Reverend H.H. Spalding and wife Eliza, and lay member W.H. Gray, who was a teacher and a mechanic. Dr. Whitman was not a minister. He had studied medicine and was practicing in his native town of Rushville, New York, when he fixed his vision on missionary work. He was of medium height with a large mouth, deep-blue eyes and distinguishing hair of dark brown and white which gave the overall effect of iron gray.

Spalding, 33 years old, was a large man with a receding hairline and a thick, full beard that hung midway down his chest. He was stern and given to outbursts of temper. Eliza was short and slender, a serious woman with a quick mind. She was strong of heart but suffered with ill-health.

Alkali Lake east of Independence Rock

The five-member missionary party arrived on the Missouri early enough in the spring of 1836 to join a band of fur traders heading west. They had with them two wagons well-loaded with provisions for the journey as well as items they would need in the future. One wagon, loaded with furniture, seeds, farm implements and most of Mr. Spalding's books, was abandoned along the Platte River. The other wagon was pulled across the Rocky Mountains to Fort Hall where it was made into a two-wheeled cart and taken on to the Hudson's Bay Company post at Fort Boise and finally given up.

The distance between Fort Boise and Fort Walla Walla was made on horseback. From there the party traveled in relative comfort in Hudson's Bay Company boats to Fort Vancouver where they were warmly welcomed. Narcissa Whitman and Eliza Spalding were the first white women to journey overland across the continent.

The women stayed at Fort Vancouver while Whitman and Spalding returned upstream to choose the sites for missions. Whitman established his twenty-five miles east of Fort Walla Walla among the Cayuse at a place he called Waiilatpu. Spalding fixed his mission 125 miles away on the Clearwater River in Nez Perce country.

Waiilatpu, meaning *Place of Rye Grass* in the Indian language, straddled the Walla Walla River. A cabin was constructed of sun-baked mud bricks and Dr. Whitman and Narcissa spent the winter in relative comfort while the Spaldings and Gray wintered at Lapwai in buffalo skin lodges.

In the spring Gray, without the approval of his associates, returned to the States where he took a wife and convinced seven friends to become missionaries. Upon reaching the Oregon country the various members of this small group scattered and missions were established among the Spokane, Nez Perce and Flathead Indians.

For a time the various missions prospered. Land was plowed and planted, churches, school houses, mills and shops were built and the Indians were taught to read and to pray. The missionary women went among the Indian lodges nursing the sick and teaching the native women to sew, cook, knit, spin and weave.

Waiilatpu was the showplace of all the missions west of the Rockies. Commodore Charles Wilkes, who was commissioned by the government to visit the Oregon country and make a report, described Waiilatpu in 1841 as composed of *"two houses, built of adobe with mud roofs, to insure a cooler habitation in summer. There were also a saw mill and some grist mills at this place, moved by water. All the premises look very comfortable. They have a fine kitchen garden, in which grow all the vegetables raised in the United States, and several kinds of fine melons. The wheat, some of which stood seven feet high, was in full head, and nearly ripe; Indian corn was in tassel, and some of it measured nine feet in height. They will reap this year about three hundred bushels of wheat, with a quantity of corn and potatoes."* The Wilkes party found the school at Waiilatpu was regularly attended by only 25 students, who collectively showed *"little disposition to improve."*

The missions seemed to be thriving, but the Indians were not being persuaded to accept the white man's God. One of the missionary wives, Mrs. Cushing Eells, wrote to her mother in March 1847: *"We have been here almost nine years, and have not yet been permitted to hear the cry of one penitent, or the songs of one redeemed soul. We often ask ourselves, why is it? Yet we labor on hoping and waiting, and expecting that the seed, though long buried, will spring up and bear fruit."*

The Indians regarded the missionaries skeptically and demanded reimbursement for land, wood and even irrigation water, claiming all had been appropriated without their permission. Gradually the Indians became bitter and contemptuous of the white people who tried to convert them from old to new beliefs. They demanded ever higher wages when asked to work and were often openly disrespectful to the missionaries. Sometimes they slipped into the kitchen at meal time and helped themselves to food as it cooked on the stove. They visited the school and disrupted the teaching.

One day Dr. Whitman ordered a troublesome Indian to leave the missionary grounds. The Indian tapped the doctor on the breastbone, and told him to hear — that the mission was Indian land and Indians could do as they pleased. Dr. Whitman pretended not to hear and the Indian grabbed his ear and twisted it. The doctor, consumed by Christian ideals, turned his head and allowed his other ear to be twisted. In spite, the Indian removed the doctor's hat and threw it in the mud. Three times Dr. Whitman retrieved it and three times, each more violently, the Indian threw it in the mud. The doctor remonstrated the Indian, saying, *"Perhaps you are playing."* The Indian grunted and promptly departed.

The harmony of the missions was disturbed by more than Indian trouble. This disturbance threatened destruction. The missionaries were fighting among themselves. Spalding had been one of Narcissa's early suitors. She had refused him and she felt he had never forgiven her. In a letter to her father dated October 14, 1840, she wrote: *"The man [Spalding] who came with us is one who never ought to have come. My dear husband has suffered more from him, in consequence of his wicked jealousy, and his great pique toward me, than can be known in this world. But he suffers not alone — the whole mission suffers, which is most to be deplored. It has nearly broken up the mission."*

At nearly every general meeting of the missionaries, differences between Spalding and Whitman were recorded and minutes of the meetings forwarded to the missionary board in Boston. The Prudential committee of the American Board, at its February meeting in 1842, voted to sharply curtail the western missionary drive. They sent a message to Whitman with Dr. Elijah White, who was leading a party of settlers west, directing that all missions except Tsimakain (near Colville, Washington), which had had some degree of success at converting the natives, be closed. If the order of the board had been carried out, the Whitmans and two other couples would have been transferred to Tsimakain while the Spaldings would have returned east.

On September 28, 1842, a meeting of all the missionaries was held at the Whitman mission to discuss the crisis confronting them. Dr. Whitman spoke, saying he believed the board had gravely erred in its judgment. He felt it his duty to start at once for the East and persuade the board to reverse its decision.

Such a journey would be perilous. Only four points along the trail were inhabited where food, clothing and additional horses could be obtained: Fort Boise, Fort Hall, the rendezvous site at Green River and Fort Laramie. Though several tried to convince Dr. Whitman to wait at least until spring, they all, in the end, signed a resolution that Whitman be given immediate liberty to visit the United States to *"confer with the committee of the American Board of Commissioners for Foreign Missions in regard to the interests of this mission."*

With the consent of his associates Whitman began making preparations for his overland journey. A. Lawrence Lovejoy, a young Massachusetts lawyer who had arrived at Waiilatpu with the White party, agreed to accompany him.

October 3, 1842, Whitman and Lovejoy departed Waiilatpu. In the next eleven days they traversed 600 miles to Fort Hall. Here they heard of Indian trouble to the east and, rather than challenging the Indians and the deep snow in the mountains, they swung south to the Great Salt Lake.

Lovejoy wrote an account of the journey: *"We suffered considerably from cold and scarcity of provisions, and for food were compelled to eat the flesh of mules, dogs and such other animals as came within our reach....Nothing occurred of much importance, other than the hard and slow traveling, until we reached, as* our guide informed us, the Grand River, which was frozen on either side about one-third across. The current was so very rapid that the center of the stream remained open, although the weather was so intensely cold. The stream was some one hundred and fifty or two hundred yards wide, and was looked upon by our guide as very dangerous to cross in its present condition. But the doctor, nothing daunted, was the first to take the water. He mounted his horse, and the guide and myself pushed them off the ice into the boiling foaming stream. Away they went completely under water, horse and all, but directly came up, and after buffeting the waves and foaming current, he made to the ice on the opposite side, a long way down the stream; leaped from his horse onto the ice, and soon had his noble animal by his side. The guide and I forced in the pack animals, followed the doctor's example, and were soon drying our frozen clothes by a comfortable fire.''

Lovejoy parted company with Dr. Whitman on the headwaters of the Arkansas River in early January 1834. A profile of Dr. Whitman appeared in the New York **Spectator** written by a fellow passenger on the steamboat: "...we also had one who was the observed of all, Dr. Whitman, the missionary from Oregon. Rarely have I seen such a spectacle as he presented. His dress should be preserved as a curiosity; it was quite in the style of the old pictures of Philip Quarles and Robinson Crusoe....he was every inch a man and no common one was clear. The Doctor has been eight years at the territory, has left his wife there, and started from home on the first of October. He had not been in bed since, having made his lodging on a buffalo robe and blanket, even on board the boat...."

Dr. Whitman reached Boston March 30, 1843, after six months of travel. He appealed for the continuation of the Oregon missions, but the American Board was more inclined to censure him for having left his station without their prior permission, but the doctor was successful. The board withdrew its order closing the missions among the Cayuse and the Nez Perce and agreed to continue support.

After winning the board's endorsement the doctor departed Boston immediately, hoping to overtake an emigrant wagon train then being formed in Independence. He joined the company of 800 and helped guide them and their ox teams to Waiilatpu, the first wagons to come west of Fort Hall. From the Whitman mission the wagon company divided into small groups and made their way to the Willamette Valley.

Following the success of this group there was an influx of more emigrants the next year. The Whitman mission served as a stopping place for the travelers. Dr. Whitman, Narcissa and the other missionaries performed a valuable service by offering a place to rest as well as sharing provisions from their garden and stock of supplies. The emigrants brought with them measles and dysentery which swept in epidemics over the Indian population. A sinister whisper among the Indians said the diseases had been introduced to exterminate the natives and acquire their lands.

And then came the fatal day of November 29, 1847. Nancy Osborne, who was a young girl at the time, recalled in later years what happened:

"A number of emigrant families had stopped for the winter, expecting to go on in the spring to the Willamette Valley. They brought the measles with them. That year the Indians had been more troublesome than usual. Many of them had the measles and their mode of treatment was nearly always fatal to the patient. They would take a sweat bath and then jump into the cold water. Of course death was the result. We also had the measles. My mother came near dying and we buried her babe on the 14th of November. My sister, in her sixth year, died on the 24th. Her memory brings to mind a scene which I cannot forget. An Indian came into the room where the form of my sister lay. Mrs. Whitman asked leave to show him the dead child. She wanted the Indians to know the measles were killing the white people as well as Indians and thus hoped to allay the growing distrust of the red men. The Indian looked long at my sister, then cruelly he laughed, to see the pale face dead. The good doctor and his noble wife were kept busy night and day to care for the sick and dying.

"At last came the fatal 29th....Three men, Messrs. Kimball, Hoffman and Canfield, were dressing a beef. Father, who had been out to get a bucket of water, remarked that there were more Indians about than usual but thought it was because they had killed the beef. Mother had gone in to Mrs. Whitman's room to see Hannah Sager and Helen Meek, who were sick with the measles. Both girls died a few days later. It was the first time that mother had walked across the room for three weeks. The Doctor, who was sitting by the stove reading, was called into the kitchen to give a sick Indian some medicine. The sudden and continuous firing of guns was the first alarm. Mrs. Whitman began to cry and the children to scream. Mother said, 'Mrs. Whitman, what is the matter?' She replied, 'The Indians are going to kill us all.' Mother came back into our room and told us what was being done. Mrs. Whitman called out to fasten the doors and father took a flat iron from the fireplace and drove a nail above the latch on the outside of our room. Then he seated himself on a box by the foot of the bed on which lay my brother, John, sick with the measles. Mother sat near the head of the bed and I was between them. Mrs. Whitman came in soon after more water. Mr. Kimball had been wounded and had fainted. She came back a second time, asked for my father, and said, 'My husband is dead and I am left a widow.' She returned to her room wringing her hands and saying, 'That Joe! That Joe! He has done it all.' This Joe Lewis was a half breed Indian of ill repute who had crossed the plains that year from the Red River country. He it was...who told the Indians that the Doctor was poisoning them. Joe Lewis and an Indian named Cup-ups came around the house and broke our window with the butts of their guns. Mrs. Whitman and those in her room had gone upstairs. I had spoken twice to father and said, 'Let's go under the floor.' He did not answer me but when the Indians began breaking in the doors of the adjoining room he opened the floor, which was made of loose boards, and we were soon concealed beneath. In a few moments our room was full of Indians, talking and laughing as if it were a holiday. The only noise made was by my brother, Alex, two years old. When the Indians came into our room and were directly over our heads, he said, 'Mother, the Indians are taking all of our things.' Hastily she clapped her hand over his mouth and whispered that he must be still. I have often been asked how I felt when under the floor. I cannot tell, but I do remember how hard my heart beat, and how large the ventilation holes in the adobe walls looked to me. They were probably only three or four inches wide and a foot long, but they seemed very large to me when I could see the Indians close on the other side. The Indians tried to follow those who had gone upstairs, but were kept back by a broken gun being pointed at them. Then they persuaded them to come down, saying that they were going to burn the house. Mrs. Whitman fainted when she came down and saw the Doctor dying. She was placed on a settee and carried by Mr. Rogers and an Indian. At the door Mr. Rogers saw the circle of Indians with their guns ready to shoot and dropping his end of the settee, exclaimed, 'My God, we are betrayed.' A volley from the waiting savages was his answer and both he and Mrs. Whitman were mortally wounded. The Indians then told Joe Lewis that if he was on their side he must kill Francis Sager, to prove it. Francis was my school mate and about fourteen years old. We heard him cry to Lewis, 'O Joe, don't shoot me,' then the crack of the gun as Lewis proved his loyalty to the red men.

"As soon as it became dark the Indians left for their lodges, of which a number were near. Everything became still. It was the stillness of death. All we could hear was the dying groans of Mr. Rogers, who lay within six feet of us. We heard him say, 'Come, Lord Jesus, come quickly.' Afterward he said faintly, 'Sweet Jesus.' Then faint and fainter came the moans until they ceased altogether. Thus died my first teacher."

The Whitman massacre is said to have begun with rumors initiated by the mixed-blood Delaware named Joe Lewis who harbored a deep hatred of the white race. He told the Cayuse Dr. Whitman was killing them with the medicine he administered for the measles and dysentery, just so he could steal the land and sell it to the steady stream of pioneers.

Under the pretense that a sick Indian needed his attention, Dr. Whitman was called to the door where he was struck on the head with a tomahawk. The Indians ran wild after that. They killed 14 people, including Dr. Whitman and Narcissa. They took 53 women and children captive.

Peter Skene Ogden was at Fort Vancouver when he learned about the massacre. Immediately he gathered a small company of men. They started east December 7, 1847, and arrived at Fort Walla Walla on the 19th. He called a council of important chiefs of neighboring tribes and informed them if they joined the Cayuse they would be killed to the last man. He concluded by offering to ransom the captives.

On December 29, for $400 worth of blankets, shirts, tobacco, guns and ammunition, Ogden purchased the release of the women and children who had suffered poor treatment while held captive by the Indians.

Provisional troops were sent to punish the guilty. They chased the Cayuse from their homeland, and by early spring 1850 the fugitive Cayuse nation was on the verge of starvation. At last five members of the tribe were brought to the settlement at The Dalles. They were transferred to Oregon City for trial. A guilty verdict was returned and the prisoners were executed June 3, 1850.

As a result of the Whitman massacre the mission at Waiilatpu was closed. The American Board of Commissioners for Foreign Missions withdrew their support and the missionary effort in Oregon was abandoned.

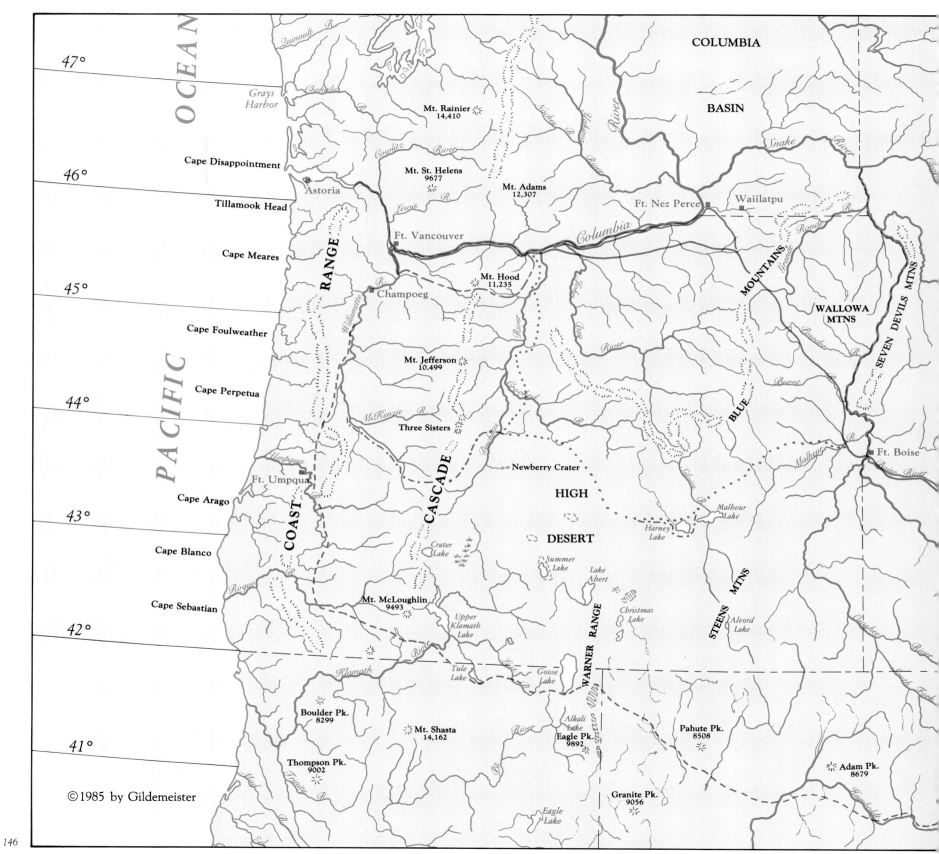

COLUMBIA

BASIN

OCEAN

Quinault R.

Grays Harbor

Chehalis R.

Cape Disappointment

Mt. Rainier
14,410

Astoria

Tillamook Head

Mt. St. Helens
9677

Mt. Adams
12,307

Ft. Nez Perce

Waiilatpu

Cowlitz River

Lewis R.

Naches R.

Yakima River

Columbia River

Snake River

Cape Meares

Ft. Vancouver

Columbia

RANGE

Willamette R.

Champoeg

Mt. Hood
11,235

Cape Foulweather

MOUNTAINS

WALLOWA
MTNS

Grande Ronde

SEVEN DEVILS MTNS

Cape Perpetua

Mt. Jefferson
10,499

BLUE

Burnt R.

PACIFIC

McKenzie R.

Three Sisters

Deschutes R.

John Day River

Cape Arago

Umpqua R.

Ft. Umpqua

Newberry Crater

HIGH

Malheur R.

Ft. Boise

Boise River

Cape Blanco

CASCADE

Crater
Lake

DESERT

Harney
Lake

Malheur
Lake

Rogue

COAST

*Summer
Lake*

Silvies R.

Cape Sebastian

Mt. McLoughlin
9493

*Upper
Klamath
Lake*

*Lake
Abert*

Christmas
Lake

STEENS MTNS

Alvord
Lake

WARNER RANGE

Klamath River

Tule
Lake

Goose
Lake

Boulder Pk.
8299

Mt. Shasta
14,162

River

*Alkali
Lake*

Eagle Pk.
9892

Pahute Pk.
8508

Thompson Pk.
9002

Pit R.

Adam Pk.
8679

©1985 by Gildemeister

Granite Pk.
9056

*Eagle
Lake*

47°
46°
45°
44°
43°
42°
41°

The Emigration Westward

The wandering explorers, trappers and traders established a path of least resistance leading from civilization up the Platte and Sweetwater rivers, over the Rocky Mountains at South Pass to Green River, Snake River, across the Blue Mountains and beyond to the Columbia River and the Willamette Valley.

Astorian Robert Stuart is credited with being the first white man over the route. He traveled from Astoria to St. Louis, taking nine months and arriving April 30, 1813. In 1832 Captain Benjamin Bonneville extended the wagon road, used by the fur companies to supply the trappers, as far as Green River. Dr. Whitman and his associates lengthened the trail even farther in 1836 when they brought their two-wheeled cart to Fort Boise.

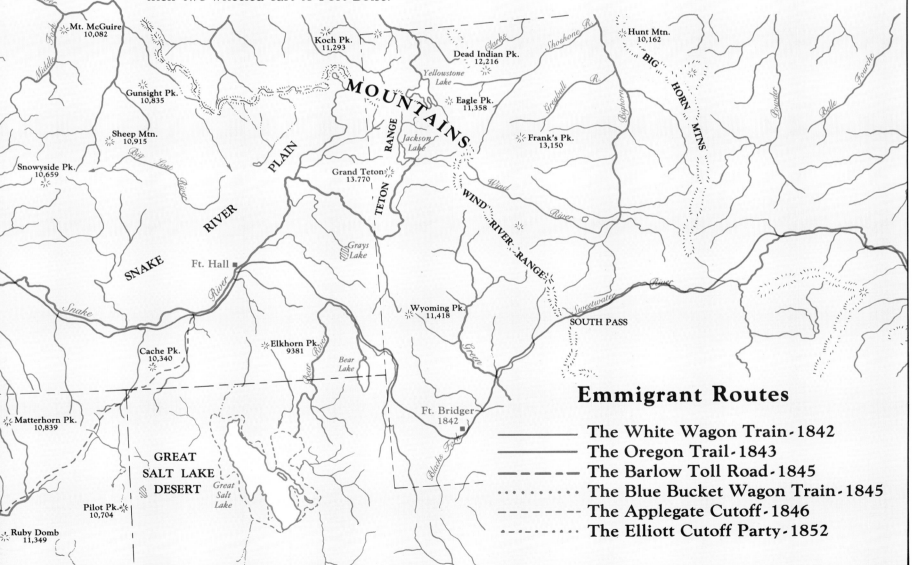

Emmigrant Routes

———————	The White Wagon Train - 1842
———————	The Oregon Trail - 1843
— — — —	The Barlow Toll Road - 1845
· · · · · · ·	The Blue Bucket Wagon Train - 1845
– – – – –	The Applegate Cutoff - 1846
-·-·-·-·	The Elliott Cutoff Party - 1852

An outgrowth of Jason Lee's return to the States to appeal for money and volunteers was the Peoria Party, a group of fourteen men led by Thomas Farnham. They departed from Peoria, Illinois, in May 1839. Along the way disagreements developed over Farnham's leadership. Men broke away, proceeding on their own, and when Farnham finally reached the Willamette Valley late that year only three men remained with him. Farnham gave up the idea of starting a colony. He returned east and wrote several books touting the trail to Oregon and the Willamette Valley. The books were well-received and helped stir interest in settling the West.

Three men took Jason Lee's appeal for missionaries to heart. In 1840 the Reverends Harvey Clark and Alvin Smith and layman P.B. Littlejohn, and their wives, started west to build a mission. They traveled with two wagons. At Green River they fell in with six trappers who were giving up on the Rocky Mountains and taking their Indian wives and children to the country they had heard so much about, the Willamette Valley.

The wagons were brought as far as Fort Hall where the missionary group gave them to the trappers in exchange for their services. The trappers realized it would be difficult to get the wagons across the sandy desert and over the mountains to the Columbia, but thinking their wives and children would be more comfortable riding they resolved to make the attempt. They departed Fort Hall August 15, 1840. One of the trappers, Robert Newell, gave an account of the undertaking: *"In a few days, we began to realize the difficult task before us, and found that the continued crashing of sage under our wagons, which was in many places higher than the mules' backs, was no joke. Seeing our animals begin to fail, we began to lighten up, finally threw away our wagon beds, and were quite sorry we had undertaken the job. All the consolation we had was that we broke the first sage on the road....In a rather rough and reduced state we arrived at Dr. Whitman's mission station, in the Walla Walla valley, where we were met by that hospitable man, and kindly made welcome, and feasted accordingly. On hearing me regret that I had undertaken to bring the wagons, the Doctor said: 'Oh, you will never regret it; you have broken the ice and when others see that wagons have passed, they too, will pass and in a few years the valley will be full of our people.' The Doctor shook me heartily by the hand."*

Powder Valley & Elkhorn Mountains

The White Wagon Train

Missionary Dr. Elijah White is often credited with opening the door to the great westward migration. He was the first to organize and start a large number of people and a caravan of wagons over the Oregon Trail.

In 1840 Dr. White was a member of the Willamette Valley Methodist Mission, but he and the Reverend Jason Lee quarreled and Lee sent him away.

Dr. White traveled east, met with Missouri Senator Lewis Linn, a strong advocate for Oregon becoming a territory, and with the Senator's help was able to win a government appointment as sub-Indian Agent to the Oregon country.

With this purely political title, Dr. White traveled extensively through the States lecturing on the Oregon Trail and vaunting the Oregon country and the opportunities that awaited the enterprising individual willing to relocate. The topics drew lively interest wherever he went and Dr. White was able to hand-pick those in the first wagon train: blacksmiths, wagon makers, road and bridge builders, farmers and merchants.

The company gathered in May 1842 at Elm Grove, Missouri. A stringent code was drafted forbidding profanity and immoral conduct; misdeeds would be enforced with reprimands, fines and finally by expulsion. The wagon train consisted of 18 ox-drawn wagons, a considerable band of horses, mules and cattle and 105 men, women and children.

The emigrants were an independent group and Dr. White's form of strict discipline was not agreeable to them. At one point, Dr. White ordered all the dogs in camp be killed rather than take the chance they might go mad in the arid plains ahead. Twenty-two dogs were shot before the owners of the remaining dogs joined together and refused to allow any more destroyed.

Eventually the members rebelled and called for a vote. Dr. White was ousted and Lansford Hastings was elected captain. A disgruntled White and his followers split from the main body and managed to stay in the lead until reaching Fort Laramie. There they were advised to reunite for the sake of safety while passing through Indian country.

The two groups traveled together and at Green River crossing some of the wagons were dismantled and used to make pack saddles. The few remaining wagons were left at Fort Hall. Again the party divided along political lines. They followed the same route across the Snake, up the Burnt river canyon into the Grande Ronde Valley and over the Blue Mountains. From there those following White went on the Hudson's Bay trail to Fort Walla Walla. The other group chose the Whitman mission at Waiilatpu where they were welcomed and given supplies.

The groups fragmented even more, with some members purchasing transportation down the Columbia in Hudson's Bay Company boats. Others went by Indian canoes and those unable to afford transportation by water struck overland, riding or walking along Indian trails.

One of the emigrants, Medorem Crawford, reported the last stretch from the Walla Walla River to Willamette Falls *"occupied about twenty days and, all things considered, was the hardest part of the journey. What with the drifting sands, rocky cliffs and rapid streams along the Columbia River, and the gorges, torrents, and thickets of the Cascade Mountains, it seems incredible how, with our worn-out and emaciated animals we ever reached our destination. On the 5th of October, our little party, tired, ragged and hungry, arrived at the falls, now Oregon City, where we found the first habitations west of the Cascade Mountains. Here several member of the Methodist mission were located. Our gratification on arriving safely, after so long and perilous journey was shared by these hospitable people, each of whom seemed anxious to give us hearty welcome, and render us every assistance in his power."*

Green River of western Wyoming

The Emigrants of 1843

Emigrants were willing to endure the hardships of the trail and take a chance on Oregon for a variety of reasons. Some were born wanderers, comfortable only in the frontier. Others were attracted by a bill being discussed in the Congress that would give American adults 640 acres and 160 acres for each child willing to go to Oregon to claim it.

A few men wanted to go for more patriotic reasons. Peter H. Burnett said: *"I saw that a great American community would grow up in the space of a few years upon the shores of the distant Pacific, and I felt an ardent desire to aid in this most important enterprise. At that same time, the country was claimed by both Great Britain and the United States, so that the most ready and peaceable way to settle the conflicting and doubtful claims of the two governments was to fill the country with American citizens. If we could only show by practical test that American emigrants could safely make their way across the continent to Oregon with their wagons, teams, cattle and families, then the solution of the question of title to the country was discovered."*

Another group of emigrants formed at Elm Grove, Missouri, in the spring of 1843. It was a large group of 1,000 men, women and children, 120 wagons and about 5,000 head of cattle. Peter Burnett was elected captain and on May 22, 1843, the wagon train started west.

From the beginning there was a problem with discipline. After only eight days Burnett resigned and William Martin was elected captain. Soon after, the expedition divided into two parts — the *light column* including the wagons and those on horseback, and the *cow column*. Jesse Applegate, who owned more livestock than any other emigrant, was elected captain of the cow column.

These divisions traveled within supporting distance of each other but maintained separate organizations. The light column led the way. Along the Platte River the pioneers were met by Dr. Whitman who was returning to his Oregon mission after pleading for support in Boston. He was welcomed into the company as an advisor because he had experience crossing the Oregon Trail when they had none. He helped choose camp sites and spent much of his time scouting the best route for the wagons, plunging his horse into streams in search of fords and meeting with bands of roving Indians. In the evenings he ministered to the sick.

One of the emigrants, James W. Nesmith, wrote: *"Dr. Marcus Whitman, in charge of the mission at Waiilatpu, in the Walla Walla Valley, was not a regular clergyman, though he sometimes preached.... While with us he was clad entirely in buckskin...he said more to us about the practical matters connected with our march than he did about theology or religious creeds...."*

The columns crossed over the Rocky Mountains at South Pass to Green River and through the parched, high desert to Snake River and Fort Hall. There the pioneers were advised by members of the Hudson's Bay Company to abandon the wagons but Dr. Whitman encouraged them to continue, telling them to take the wagons on to the Columbia.

South Pass & Wind River Mountains

Many emigrants chose to rely upon Dr. Whitman's judgment, others shifted to pack trains and made much better time crossing the Snake and threading their way up the rocky confines of Burnt river canyon. Dr. Whitman guided the wagon caravan until nearing the Blue Mountains and then he went ahead to his mission to prepare for the emigrants' reception.

Jesse Applegate, son of Lindsay Applegate and nephew of Captain Jesse Applegate — a seven-year-old at the time — later wrote his recollections of the experience: *"We descended a long steep hill into*

Sisley Creek of the Burnt River Canyon

Grande Ronde Valley, so late in the evening that we had no view of the valley as we went down and camped on or near a small river. The morning came clear and quite cool and we found ourselves in a fine valley probably fifteen miles long and wide enough to be called round. Early in the morning, soon after sunrise, looking in a northerly direction several miles away we could see a column of steam arising from the ground like a white cloud. This they said was from a hot spring or small lake. I think I fancied this was quite a good country, though it was then inhabited by Indians only.

Grande Ronde Valley

Blue Mountain Crossing

"Some things of the crossing of the Blue Mountains I remember quite well. The timber had to be cut and removed to make a way for the wagons. The trees were cut just near enough to the ground to allow the wagons to pass over the stumps, and the road through the forest was only cleared out wide enough for the wagon to pass along...."

"In passing across these mountains, we were overtaken by a snow storm which made the prospects very dismal. I remember wading through mud and snow and suffering from the cold and wet. But the camp on the Umatilla was a very pleasant place; this we soon reached after passing the mountains. The Umatilla was a small stream with sandy banks and bottom. About the stream were quaking asp and black haws. I distinctly remember noticing the quaking asp trees here for the first time. A camp fire on the bank of the creek was burning near one of these trees and as the sparks and smoke went up, the great wriggling among the leaves attracted my attention as I lay on my back looking up into its foliage...."

"...Journeying from our camp on the Umatilla, we passed across what seemed to me to be a kind of sandy desert, with at times rocky ground, sage brush, greasewood, and occasionally a few willows.

"We passed Whitman's Mission; situated in about such a country as last above described. There was nothing cheerful or inviting about the place; a low and very modest looking house or two, the doctor in the yard and one or two other persons about the premises, are about all I remember of this historic place where the slaughter was to be three years later. I think we did not halt here, but just passed along by the place...."

The company broke apart at Whitman's mission. Some went on horseback or afoot along the Indian trail hugging the south bank of the Columbia River. The families of the Applegate brothers, Jesse, Charles and Lindsay, and ten families and twenty wagons faithful to them, chose to travel to Fort Walla Walla. They spent several weeks there sawing lumber and building small flat-bottomed boats. The wagons were left behind.

According to Jesse Applegate's recollections: "I well remember our start down the river, and how I enjoyed riding in the boat, the movement of which was like a grape vine swing. Shoving out from the Walla Walla canoe landing about the first of November our little fleet of boats began the voyage down the great 'River of the West.' Whirlpools looking like deep basins in the river, the lapping, splashing, and rolling of waves, crested with foam sometimes when the wind was strong, alarmed me for a day or two on the start. But I soon recovered from this childish fear, and as I learned that the motion of the boat became more lively and gyratory, rocking from side to side, leaping from wave to wave, or sliding down into a trough and then mounting with perfect ease to the crest of a wave, dashing the spray into our faces when we were in rough water, the sound of rapids and the sight of foam and white caps ahead occasioned only pleasant anticipation. Often when the current was strong, the men would rest on their oars and allow the boats to be swept along by the current...."

"Now of nights we encamped on the bank of the river, sometimes on the north, and sometimes on the south shore. I remember especially a camp we made on the south shore. There was a very narrow strip of sand and rock almost level, between the river and a high bluff, with a high mountain rising above it. Here we were, I will remember, with this precipitous bluff and lofty mountain at our back, and the broad river before us....There was a driftwood camp-fire burning and the women folks were about it doing the kitchen work and talking. I don't remember what they said except that my Aunt Cynthia, Uncle Jesse Applegate's wife, said, 'There is going to be a death in the family,' or words to that effect. She was standing, and pointing upward, added, 'See that raven flying over the camp?' I was lying upon the sand, and hearing the remark, looked up and saw a black bird, a raven or crow, flying about one hundred feet above us and going in the direction of the river. Now this thing of reading the future from the flight of birds was then new to me, and as my aunt's countenance, gesture, and tone of voice, bespoke alarm and distress, the event made a lasting impression upon my mind....

"...At the head of a rapid we were now approaching the river bears from a west course a little northerly, making a very gradual curve. As we approached this bend I could hear the sound of rapids and presently the boat began to rise and fall and rock from side to side. When we began to make the turn I could see breakers ahead extending in broken lines across the river, and the boat began to sweep along at a rapid rate. There were now breakers on the right and on the left, and occasionally foam-crested waves swept across our bows....Our boat now was about twenty yards from the right-hand shore; when looking across the river I saw a smaller boat about opposite us near the south bank. The persons in this boat were Alexander McClellan, a man about seventy years old, William Parker, probably twenty-one, and William Doke, about the same age, and three boys; Elisha Applegate, aged about eleven, and Warren and Edward Applegate, each about nine years old...presently there was a wail of anguish, a shriek, and a scene of confusion in our boat that no language can describe. The boat we were watching disappeared and we saw the man and boys struggling in the water. Father and Uncle Jesse, seeing their children drowning, were seized with frenzy, and dropping their oars, sprang up from their seats and were about to leap from the boat to make a desperate attempt to swim to them, when mother and Aunt Cynthia, in voices that were distinctly heard above the roar of the rushing waters, by commands and entreaties brought them to a realization of our own perilous situation, and the madness of an attempt to reach the other side of the river by swimming. This was sixty-seven years ago, and yet the words of that frantic appeal by the women, which saved our boat and two families from speedy and certain destruction, are fresh in my memory. They were, 'Men, don't quit the oars. If you do we will all be lost.' The men returned to the oars just in time to avoid, by great exertion, a rock against which the current dashed with such fury that the foam and froth upon its apex was as white as milk. I sat on the right-hand side of the boat and the rock was so near that I thought if we had not passed so quickly I might have put my hand upon it.

"Having escaped the present danger, the next thought, no doubt, was to effect a landing at the earliest possible moment, but the shore was rock-bound, rising several feet perpendicularly and presenting a serried line of ragged points against which the rapid current fretted and frothed, and the waves, rearing their foam-flecked heads aloft, rushed to destruction like martial squadrons upon an invincible foe. Ah! That half hour's experience, this scene so wild, so commotional, so fearful and exciting, had not death been there, were worth a month of ordinary life....

"From the south shore of the river there was a level tract of ground running back to the hill probably fifty yards wide. Indians were seen there, a few mounted on ponies, and some in canoes along the shore, and were seen to put out after the floating bedding, clothes, and various articles of furniture from the foundered boat. It was said the Indians did not make any attempt or show any desire to assist our people in the water. William Doke could not swim and had taken hold of a feather bedtick which carried him safely to the foot of the rapids, between which and what was called the main Dalles there was a short interval of quiet water. Here Mr. Doke floated clinging to the bedtick. The Indians passed by him in their canoes, and though he called for help, they did not offer any assistance. He was picked up by one of our boats as he was about to enter the second rapids....

"The boy Warren was never seen nor heard of after the boat went down the first time. The old man McClellan was seen the last time trying to reach the head of an island. He had placed the boy Edward on a couple of oars and carrying him this way, was trying to reach shore, but being hampered with a heavy coat and boots, falling a little short of the point he attempted to reach, the old man and boy disappeared under projecting cliffs and were seen no more. The brave old soldier could have saved himself by abandoning the boy, but this he would not do. Of the three persons drowned no body could be found, and the search had to be given up. The boat was never seen after it went down into the roaring throat of the second whirlpool."

The women and children hiked over the portage trail around the worst of the rapids while the men took to the oars and successfully brought the remaining scows through the churning water.

They journeyed downriver to the mouth of the Willamette and paddled against the current to the falls at Oregon City. A French-Canadian with one yoke of long-horned steers hauled the boats around the falls. At Champoeg they pulled the boats on shore and started overland to the abandoned site of the original Methodist mission.

According to the recollections of Jesse Applegate: *"We called this place the Old Mission....There were three log cabins under one roof. We went into them on the 29th day of November, 1843, and here we passed our first winter in Oregon. It was our home until after harvest the following summer.*

"Previous to this we had been in the rain most of the time for twenty days. Oh! how we could have enjoyed our hospitable shelter if we could have looked around the family circle and beheld the bright faces that had accompanied us on our toilsome journey almost to the end. Alas, they were not there!"

Columbia River Gorge

Foggy Morning

The Applegate Cutoff Trail

Lindsay Applegate wrote a memoir of his days spent in the Oregon country. Of the first winter he said: *"That long and dreary winter, with its pelting rains and howling winds, brought sadness to us. Under these sad reflections, we resolved if we remained in the country to find a better way for others who might wish to emigrate, as soon as we could possibly afford the time. From what information we could gather from old pioneers and the Hudson's Bay Co., the Cascade mountains to the south became very low, or terminated where the Klamath cut that chain; and knowing that the Blue mountains lay east and west, we came to the conclusion there must be a belt of country extending east towards the South Pass of the Rocky mountains, where there might be no very lofty ranges of mountains to cross. So in 1846, after making arrangements for subsistence of our families during our absence, we organized a company to undertake the enterprise....Each man had his pack-horse and saddle-horse, making thirty animals to guard and take care of.*

"A portion of the country we proposed to traverse was at that time marked on the map 'unexplored region'. All the information we could get relative to it was through the Hudson's Bay Co. Peter Ogden, an officer of that company, who had led a party of trappers through that region, represented that portions of it were desert-like....He also stated that portions of the country through which we would have to travel were infested with fierce and war-like savages, who would attack every party entering their country....The idea of opening a wagon road through such a country at that time, was counted as preposterous. These statements, though based on facts, we thought might be exaggerated by the Hudson's Bay Co., in their own interest, since they had a line of forts on the Snake River route, reaching from Fort Hall to Vancouver, and were prepared to profit by the immigration.

"One thing which had much influence with us was the fact that the question as to which power, Great Britain or the United States, would eventually secure a title to the country, was not settled, and in case a war should occur and Britain proved successful, it was important to have a way by which we could leave the country without running the gauntlet of the Hudson's Bay Co.'s forts and falling prey to Indian tribes which were under British influence.

Umpqua River

"On the morning of the 20th of June, 1846, we gathered near where Dallas now stands, moved up the valley and encamped for the night on Mary's River, near where the town Corvallis has since been built...."

June 22: "This day we traveled along the base of the Calapooias, our course being nearly southeast, passing near a prominent peak since called Spencer's Butte."

June 23: "We moved on through the grassy oak hills and narrow valleys to the north Umpqua River. The crossing was a rough and dangerous one, as the river bed was a mass of loose rocks, and, as we were crossing, our horses occasionally fell, giving the riders a severe dunking...."

June 27: "...Indians hovered around us all night, frightening our horses a number of times. From the tracks we could see that they approached very closely to our encampment. Making an early start we moved on very cautiously. Whenever the trail passed through the cuts we dismounted and led our horses, having our guns in hand ready at any moment to use them in self-defense, for we had adopted this rule, never to be the aggressor. Traveling through a very broken country the sharp hills separated by little streams upon which there were small openings, we came out at about noon into a large creek, a branch of Rogue River...."

June 29: "We passed over a low range of hills, from the summit of which we had a splendid view of the Rogue River valley. It seemed like a great meadow, interspersed with groves of oaks, which appeared like vast orchards...."

July 4: "...After crossing the summit of the Cascade ridge, the descent was, in places, very rapid. At noon we came out into a glade where there was water and grass and from which we could see the Klamath River. After noon we moved down through an immense forest, principally of yellow pine, to the river, and then traveled up the north bank, still through yellow pine forests, for about six miles, when all at once we came out in full fiew of the Klamath country, extending eastward as far as the eye could reach. It was an exciting moment, after the many days spent in the dense forest and among the mountains, and the whole party broke forth in cheer after cheer...."

July 7: "We left the valley of Tule Lake to pursue our course eastward, over a rocky table land, among scattering juniper trees...."

July 8: "...We found the country still quite level, but exceedingly rocky; for eight or ten miles almost like pavement. Late in the afternoon we came out into the basin of a lake [Goose Lake]...we came to a little stream coming in from the mountains to the eastward. The grass and water being good, we encamped for the night. Game seemed plentiful, and one of the party killed a fine deer in the vicinity of the camp. From a spur of the mountains, near our camp, we had a splendid view of the lake and of the extensive valley bordering it on the north...."

The Applegate party passed Goose Lake continuing south and camped on Lassen Creek. They picked a route east through a gap in the mountain wall and entered Surprise Valley in northern California. From there they found their way across the Black Rock Desert and ascended the Humboldt River before finally reaching Fort Hall.

A large wagon train was gathered at Fort Hall. The Oregon men were able to persuade about 150 emigrant families to take the southern route. The wagons cut off the Oregon Trail at Thousand Springs on August 9. Lindsay Applegate and a group of volunteers went ahead to try to improve the trail. Crossing the desert there was insufficient food for the livestock and never enough water. The wagon train was delayed and found itself, after skirmishing with the Modoc Indians, climbing the Cascade Mountains with winter approaching.

On November 9 in the canyon of the Umpqua, J. Quinn Thornton, a member of the party who kept a detailed diary, wrote: *"Having at various times upon the journey from Ogden's river [Humboldt] thrown away my property, I had little remaining save our buffalo robes, blankets, arms, ammunition, watch, and the most valuable part of our wardrobe. We were very weak in consequence of want of sufficient and healthful food. The road was very muddy and the rain was descending in the gorge of the mountains, where we were, while the snow was falling far above us upon the sides. There was a close canyon, some three miles ahead of us, down which we would have to wade three miles in cold mountain snowwater...."*

The procession of wagons straggled through the canyon, each family fending for itself as well as it could. Thornton found himself near the rear. *"We passed many wagons,"* he wrote, *"that had been abandoned by their owners, in consequence of their proprietors finding it impossible to take them over. We passed household and kitchen furniture, beds and bedding, books, carpets, cooking utensils, dead cattle, broken wagons and wagons not broken, but, nevertheless, abandoned. In short, the whole road presented the appearance of a defeated and retreating army having passed over it...."*

The hungry, the sick and the weak dropped farther back. Some stopped, lay down and died. When the first members of the expedition stumbled into the Willamette Valley the settlers there generously sent a pack train into the mountains to save the stragglers.

Umpqua Mountains

Mt. Hood

The Barlow Toll Road

Samuel K. Barlow was captain of a wagon train which arrived in The Dalles late in September 1845. Rather than abandon the wagons or ferry them down the Columbia River, Barlow led 19 people driving seven wagons and their livestock in search of a route over the Cascades.

Barlow said that: *"God never made a mountain that he did not make a place for some man to go over it or under it. I am going to hunt for that place...."*

With a small detachment of men, Barlow cut a trail through the dense forest to the summit of the Cascade Mountains at a point between Mount Hood and Mount Wilson. Here winter trapped the party. The oxen and horses were converted to pack animals, but the snow continued and the party was saved only after Dr. McLoughlin learned of their fate and sent relief.

The following spring Barlow, in partnership with Philip Foster and a crew of forty men, carved a road linking the Willamette Valley with the Oregon Trail. He used the general route of the trail he had blazed the previous year. The east end began at Tygh Valley and followed an Indian trail 85 miles over the Cascade Mountains to Foster Road and Oregon City. Swampy areas were bridged with corduroy logs and the grade was improved with pick and shovel. But the road, because of the rugged terrain, was never much better than a trail. The worst section was a particularly steep decline on the west side of the mountains called Laurel Hill. Here the drivers had to rough-lock the wagon wheels and drag a tree behind as a brake to slow the descent, or use a standing tree as a dead-head and lower the wagons with rope.

The Barlow Toll Road was completed early enough in 1846 to allow the passage of 145 wagons, 1,559 horses, mules and cattle, and one band of sheep through the toll gate. The following year many of the 5,000 emigrants who came over the Oregon Trail chose the Barlow Trail, paying a toll of $1 per head for stock and $5 per wagon.

Barlow Toll Road

High Desert Dunes

The Blue Bucket Wagon Train

In spring 1845, at the Oregon Encampment on the Missouri River, a wagon train was organized with 800 men, women and children in ox-drawn wagons and 2,000 head of stock. The trip from Missouri was uneventful until the last crossing of the Snake River. Here the leaders were persuaded by frontiersman Stephen Meek to have him guide them on a shortcut to the Willamette Valley.

Meek was the only member of the train familiar with interior Oregon, but east of the John Day River he lost his direction. The emigrants wandered into the high desert, country so desolate even the Indians avoided it. Meek stumbled into the Harney Basin and when at last they came to water, it was alkaline. They drank anyway and soon a fever epidemic struck. The children and the already sick and weak were first to die. Graves were dug beside the trail and the survivors, thirsty and near starvation, continued to Crooked River.

Bitterness against Meek became so intense that he was compelled to travel beyond rifle range. He rode on to The Dalles and sent back a relief party. In the meantime, the emigrants had given up trying to find a pass through the Cascades and had turned north. They camped on the Deschutes Rim, at Sagebrush Springs and at Hay Creek. On the long grade leading to Shaniko Flats they had to double team. From the plateau they traveled down Buck Hollow and ferried themselves and indispensable goods across the Deschutes River on an aerial tramway fashioned from a wagon box suspended with a rope.

They arrived in The Dalles in mid-October. Twenty people had died on the way and others were so weakened they died shortly after reaching the Willamette Valley.

Legend has it that at one point in the agonizing trip, several children were sent to a nearby stream to fetch water in a blue bucket. On their errand they collected a handful of pretty yellow rocks. Later it was discovered the rocks were gold nuggets and though members of the wagon train tried to retrace their route, the Blue Bucket Mine was never discovered.

Malheur River Valley

Alkali Hills of the Malheur

The Elliott Cutoff Party

The spring of 1852 a group of southern Willamette Valley homesteaders set out to discover a new route over the Oregon Cascades. They located a pass south of Diamond Peak and a road construction contract was let for twelve dollars a mile. Work started immediately.

The following year homesteader Elijah Elliott decided to travel east to meet his family coming with a wagon train. He joined them at Fort Boise and prepared to take them home over the new route. When others heard of this cutoff that would save three weeks and several hundred miles of rugged travel, they asked Elliott if he would guide them, too.

There were 1,027 people, 250 wagons and much livestock in the party that turned off the Oregon Trail and started over the same disasterous route that the Meek party had taken. In the Harney Lake region members of the wagon train had differences of opinion on which route should be taken. Some chose to skirt south around the lake; others went north, trying to follow the still-visible, erratic ruts the Meek train had made eight years earlier.

They wandered the high desert across windswept flats dotted with sagebrush, the alkaline dust burning their eyes. They were completely lost except for the bearings they took on the distant string of snow-capped peaks, the Cascades. To them the mountains were an elusive dream of trees, shade, cold spring water, plump berries and green grass for the stock.

As the travelers became more desperate, the wagon train was reformed and scouts were sent out to locate the best route to the trail head over the Southern Cascades. Andrew McClure was with the scouting party that crossed the Deschutes River (near today's Bend) and entered the mountains. He kept a diary and on October 2, 1852, wrote: *"Our guides have come to the conclusion that we did not pass around the foot of Diamond's Peak, as was intended, but being mistaken in the mountain, passed between two of the Sisters and north of the intended pass 40 or 50 miles. Surely no part of the mountains can be more rugged than we passed over."*

The scouts remained disoriented in the mountains while the wagon emigrants drew nearer, following a string of occasional blazes leading through red-barked ponderosa forests to the east face of the Cascades. The wagons reached Middle Fork Pass, south of Diamond Peak, and an indifferent road slashed through the timber was located. The progress was slow as trees had to be felled. A winter storm hit and it snowed, adding to the fear they would be trapped in the mountains — just as the Donner party had been trapped in the blizzardy Sierras during the winter of 1846-1847.

Martin Blanding, a young schoolteacher, borrowed a mule and rode for help. He followed the Middle Fork of the Willamette River and one night made camp at the base of a rounded butte (Butte Disappointment near Lowell). In the morning he was discovered by a boy from the settlement who smelled his campfire smoke and investigated.

A relief party was quickly organized and sent into the mountains where they found the members of the wagon train facing starvation. Wood was added to the campfires, griddles put on the coals and heaps of golden pancakes were cooked until not a person remained hungry.

The Elliott wagon train came through, saved by the generosity of their new neighbors. The Willamette Pass over the Cascades had been opened.

Cascade Mountain Crossing

Willamette Valley

Forming a Government

The Oregon country embraced all land west of the Rocky Mountains, north of the 42nd parallel and south of 54 degrees, 40 minutes, north. It was disputed ground jointly occupied by Great Britain and the United States under terms agreed to by the countries in 1818. Citizens and subjects of the two countries were to have free and equal access to the region.

The claim of the United States to Oregon rested with the discovery of the Columbia River by Robert Gray in 1792, the exploration of the Lewis and Clark Expedition which reached the mouth of the Columbia River in 1805, and the founding of Astoria by the Pacific Fur Company in 1811.

But Great Britain had prior claim beginning with Sir Francis Drake's voyage of discovery in 1578, Alexander Mackenzie's overland crossing to the Pacific in 1793 and the explorations of men such as Captain Cook, Captain Vancouver and Lieutenant Broughton.

The United States' control of the Columbia River, vested in the Pacific Fur Company, was lost by the sale of Fort Astoria and its scattered outposts to the North West Company in 1813. Eight years later the North West Company was merged with the Hudson's Bay Company, and three years after that Dr. John McLoughlin arrived to take charge.

As Chief Factor he was the ruler and protector of the white man and the Indian alike. When American trappers and traders arrived Dr. McLoughlin welcomed them hospitably, but refused to sell them supplies because the Company did not want competition in collecting the region's furs. When American missionaries arrived Dr. McLoughlin welcomed them, too, and sold them supplies because they were not rivals.

In the early days the Hudson's Bay Company was bound not to discharge any of its employees in the Indian country but to return them to the places of original hire. When several French-Canadian trappers, whose service was about to end, expressed their desire not to return to Canada but to settle in Oregon, Dr. McLoughlin agreed to accommodate them. He kept them on the Company's books, sold them supplies and purchased their wheat. A group of these men and their Indian wives settled in the Willamette Valley at a place that became known as French Prairie near Champoeg.

By the early 1840s there were a few Americans farming in the Willamette Valley, leftovers from the Astorians, the Wyeth expedition or free trappers. There were also the missionaries, many of whom made Oregon their permanent home; but for the most part the Americans were men who had spent years trapping and living among the Indians before settling in the Willamette Valley. They were independent and not accustomed to taking orders. They lived in the shadow of the Hudson's Bay Company, but Dr. McLoughlin was respectful of their rights.

As more Americans drifted into the country and settled, they were of a different mind. They chose not to be under the domination of the Company and petitioned the Congress, asking that the infant colony of Americans be protected by the United States. The Congress answered that it could take no action under the terms of the convention for joint occupancy.

The Americans residing in the Willamette Valley were determined, and on February 7, 1841, a meeting was called at Champoeg. The call was cautiously worded to avoid the question of national sovereignty. Nothing was accomplished at the meeting beyond forming a committee to draft a code of laws for the government of the country.

On February 15 an event occurred which accelerated action. Ewing Young, a native of Tennessee and frontiersman in Mexico and California, had become the most prosperous American settler in Oregon. He died suddenly February 15, 1841, leaving considerable stock and property but no legal claimants or known heirs. Since there was no probate court the administration of the property became a perplexing question.

Young was buried on the 17th. The funeral was attended by a large number of settlers who held a meeting after the services. It was decided that a committee of seven be elected to draft a constitution and code of laws for the government of the region south of the Columbia River. If any settlers north of the Columbia, not connected with the Hudson's Bay Company, petitioned, they, too, would be included.

But the committee was split along political and ecclesiastical lines. The question of whether Oregon was to be governed by British or American rule; and whether the Protestant missionary, the Catholic missionary, or the strongly individual non-church element was going to have the strongest voice; split the group. The result was no action.

The question of government simmered as more Americans began to arrive over the Oregon Trail and settle in the Willamette Valley. Early in 1843 the Provisional Government was again brought to the forefront, this time under the cloak of what afterward became known as the Wolf Meeting.

The Wolf Meeting was scheduled for the first Monday in March 1843. Its purpose was to adopt measures for the protection of domestic animals from wild ones. Resolutions were adopted relative to paying bounties for killing wolves and other dangerous wild animals.

Before the meeting was adjourned a resolution was adopted which read: *That a Committee be appointed to take into consideration the propriety of taking measures for the civil and military protection of this colony.* This action led to the dramatic meeting of May 2, 1843.

The majority of Willamette Valley settlers attended that meeting and seemed evenly split between French-Canadians and Americans. Each side had been coached in advance to vote no on every question or motion proposed by the opposition.

In an open meadow dotted with oak trees, a motion was made for the establishment of a Provisional Government. During a spirited debate it appeared the gathering was evenly divided. At last one of the Americans, mountain man Joe Meek who was dressed that day in buckskins, decided the timing was right to demand a vote. He jumped to his feet and growled, *"Who's for a divide? All in favor...follow me!"* The fate of Oregon hung in the balance. Would the country be affiliated with the United States as the Americans wanted or would it be affiliated with Great Britain as the French-Canadians wanted?

Joe Meek stepped to the right of an imaginary dividing line and 49 others moved to stand with him. Across the line were 52 French-Canadians.

Among the French-Canadians was Francois Xavier Matthieu who had taken an active role against Great Britain during the Canadian rebellion of 1837-1838. After the failure of the revolt Matthieu left Canada. He came west with the White wagon train of 1842 and spent his first winter in the Willamette Valley with the family of Etienne Lucier, a member of the Astor party.

Lucier, like most of the French-Canadians, was apprehensive about being controlled by any government and particularly fearful of unnecessary laws and excessive taxation. He had been told windows were taxed in the States and was convinced the openings in his own log cabin would be a luxury he could not afford if the Americans won.

Matthieu informed him this was not the case and made convincing arguments against what he considered the tyranny of the British in Canada. He touted the government of the United States, saying its laws were just and liberal and all men were treated equally.

For a moment it appeared the French-Canadians had won by a margin of 52 to 50. Then Matthieu stepped to the American side, followed by Lucier. Joe Meek threw his hat in the air and called, *"Three cheers for our side!"*

Three cheers rang out. The defeated French-Canadians quickly mounted their horses and departed, leaving the meadow to the joyful Americans. So began the first government in the Oregon country.

In 1846 the 49th parallel was established as the boundary with Canada, and two years later the Congress officially recognized Oregon as a territory. Later this area was carved into states: Oregon, admitted as the 33rd state February 14, 1859; Montana, the 41st state admitted November 8, 1889; Washington, the 42nd state on November 11, 1889; Idaho, the 43rd state on July 3, 1890; and Wyoming, admitted as the 44th state July 10, 1890.

Long ago a seed borne on the wind came to rest on the bank of the Willamette River. Soft rain fell, the seed sprouted and took hold in the deep, fertile soil. Over the centuries explorers, traders, trappers, missionaries and pioneers passed along a nearby Indian trail and sometimes stopped to take refuge from the elements under the umbrella of protection offered by the big tree.

Today the tree is surrounded by a carpet of wild flowers and delicate ferns, moss clings to the massive trunk and wide-set, leafy branches cut a tremendous arc across the sky. This monarch is a living sentinel, spanning the recorded history of the great Oregon country.

Bigleaf Maple at Champoeg

Historical Notes of the Oregon Country

Chronological History of the Oregon Country

1542 - Spaniard Bartolome Ferrelo sails as far north as the southwest coast of Oregon.

1578 - Englishman Sir Francis Drake sails along the Pacific Northwest coast.

1603 - Spaniard Martin de Aguilar sails along the coast and discovers evidence of a great river in the vicinity of where the Columbia River was later discovered.

1742 - Frenchman Pierre Gaultier de Varennes (Sieur de la Verendrye) becomes the first European to see the Rocky Mountains.

1765 - First published use of the Indian name Oregon (or Ouragon) by Major Robert Rogers, in a petition to King George III.

1774 - Spaniard Juan Perez sails to 54 degrees, 40 minutes, north.

1775 - Spaniard Bruno Heceta makes note of a great river in the vicinity of 46 degrees, north.

1778 - Englishman James Cook visits the Northwest coast on a voyage of discovery. His crew opens the sea otter trade with China.

1787 - Englishman Charles Barkley sails into and names Strait of Juan de Fuca.

1792 - May 11 - American Robert Gray discovers and enters the Columbia River, giving it his ship's name.

1792 - October - Englishman W.R. Broughton explores the Columbia River.

1793 - July - Scotchman Alexander Mackenzie is the first European to cross the North American continent.

1803 - Louisiana Purchase brings United States territory to the summit of the Rocky Mountains.

1804 - Americans Lewis and Clark start an expedition to the mouth of the Columbia River.

1806 - Lewis and Clark complete expedition and return to St. Louis.

1807 - Simon Fraser discovers the Fraser River.

1810 - June 1 - American Nathan Winship arrives at the Columbia River in his ship *Albatross* and attempts to establish a colony at Oak Point, but the colony fails.

1811 - March 22 - John Jacob Astor's ship *Tonquin* arrives at the mouth of the Columbia River and the Pacific Fur Company soon after erects Fort Astoria, the first successful settlement in the Pacific Northwest.

1811 - April - Wilson Price Hunt and the Astor overland expedition departs winter quarters on the Missouri River and starts west.

1811 - July - The *Tonquin*, anchored at Clayoquot harbor on Vancouver Island, is attacked by natives; the captain and crew are murdered and the ship blown up.

1811 - July 15 - David Thompson of the North West Company travels the length of the Columbia River and is disappointed to find the Americans have established Fort Astoria and already laid claim to the territory.

1811 - July 23 - David Stuart and a small party head up the Columbia River to establish Fort Okanogan. Alexander Ross is put in charge.

1812 - Robert Stuart and company depart Astoria for New York with dispatches for Astor. South Pass is discovered over the Rocky Mountains and will later be the route of the Oregon Trail.

1812 - War with Great Britain.

1813 - October 23 - Fort Astoria is sold to the North West Company and renamed Fort George.

1813 - October 29 - British warship *Raccoon* enters the Columbia.

1814 - First livestock in the Pacific Northwest is brought by ship from California.

1818 - Fort Nez Perce, later renamed Fort Walla Walla, is established near the mouth of the Walla Walla River on the east bank of the Columbia River.

1818 - The United States and Great Britain sign a treaty of joint occupancy in the Pacific Northwest.

1819 - Treaty with Spain fixes southern boundary of the Oregon country at 42 degrees, north. All Spanish claims north are released to the United States.

1821 - The North West Company merges with the Hudson's Bay Company under the name of the latter.

1824 - Treaty with Russia fixes the northern boundary of the Oregon country at 54 degrees, 40 minutes, north.

1824 - Dr. John McLoughlin appointed chief factor of the Columbia District.

1825 - March 19 - Fort Vancouver dedicated by the Hudson's Bay Company.

1825 - Peter Skene Ogden explores and traps eastern and central Oregon.

1827 - First sawmill in the Pacific Northwest built at Fort Vancouver.

1828 - First gristmill in the Pacific Northwest built at Fort Vancouver.

1828 - July - Jedediah Smith expedition massacred on the Umpqua River.

1829 - Hudson's Bay post established at Willamette Falls.

1830 - John Work takes over from Peter Skene Ogden as chief trader for the Hudson's Bay Company.

1831 - Four Indians travel to St. Louis seeking missionaries to come to the Oregon country.

1832 - Hudson's Bay Company establishes a fort on the Umpqua River.

1832 - Nathaniel Wyeth travels to the Columbia on his first expedition.

1833 - First school in the Pacific Northwest established at Fort Vancouver. First teacher is John Ball, a member of the Wyeth party.

1833 - First logs exported from Oregon to China.

1834 - March 4 - Captain Bonneville reaches Fort Walla Walla and his request to purchase supplies is denied.

1834 - Nathaniel Wyeth, on his second expedition, establishes Fort Hall on the Snake River.

1834 - Jason Lee preaches the first sermon west of the Rockies. The Willamette Mission begins.

1836 - Dr. Marcus Whitman and associates bring a two-wheeled cart as far west as Fort Hall. Protestant missions are started at Waiilatpu and Lapwai.

1839 - First group of settlers, the Peoria Party, arrives in Oregon.

1841 - The *Star of Oregon*, first ship built by Americans in the Oregon country, is launched on the Willamette River.

1842 - May 16 - White wagon train departs Elm Grove, Missouri. Wagons brought as far as Fort Hall.

1842 - Willamette University, the first university west of the Mississippi, is founded by Jason Lee.

1843 - May 2 - Provisional government in the Oregon country is established at Champoeg.

1843 - Emigrants bring wagons as far as Fort Walla Walla. Approximately 900 settlers arrive in the Willamette Valley.

1843 - John C. Fremont, with guides Kit Carson and Billy Chinook, traverses Oregon east of the Cascades.

1845 - June 3 - Provisional government revised. George Abernethy is elected provisional governor.

1845 - The *Lost Wagon Train* wanders across the Oregon high desert.

1846 - Treaty between the United States and Great Britain establishes the Oregon boundary at 49 degrees, north.

1847 - November 29 - Whitman massacre at Waiilatpu. The first Indian war, the Cayuse War follows.

1848 - August 14 - Oregon Territory established by the Congress. Abraham Lincoln is asked to be governor of the Oregon Territory but declines.

1849 - March 3 - General Joseph Lane, first appointed governor of Oregon Territory, takes office.

1850 - Donation Land Claim Law is enacted. Mail service between the Willamette Valley and San Francisco is established. Rogue River Indian War begins.

1853 - Washington Territory is created from the northern portion of the Oregon Territory.

1853 - The Elliott Cutoff Party becomes lost on the high desert of eastern and central Oregon.

1855 - The Yakima Indian War begins. The first telegraph is operated in Oregon.

1856 - Because of the Indian wars, eastern Oregon and Washington are closed to settlement by Army order.

1857 - August and September - Constitutional convention held at Salem. Constitution ratified by popular vote.

1858 - John Whiteaker elected first governor of Oregon.

1859 - February 14 - Oregon admitted as the 33rd state.

1860 - Stagecoach service inaugurated between Portland and Sacramento.

1863 - Idaho Territory created.

1864 - Salem becomes the Oregon State Capitol by popular vote.

1872 - The Modoc Indian War.

1877 - The Nez Perce Indian War.

1878 - The Bannock Indian War.

1883 - The transcontinental railroad linking the Northwest to the other sections of the country is completed.

1887 - Oregon-California railroad is completed.

1889 - November 8 - Montana admitted as the 41st state.

1889 - November 11 - Washington admitted as the 42nd state.

1890 - July 3 - Idaho admitted as the 43rd state.

1890 - July 10 - Wyoming admitted as the 44th state.

Beacon Rock on the Columbia River

Oregon Country Biographies

The Pacific Northwest was a remote, undiscovered corner of the world until Sir Francis Drake stumbled upon it searching for a way back to the Atlantic Ocean. In later years Spanish sea captains arrived hoping to discover the fabled Northwest Passage but they found the rocky coastline continued without interruption. It was not until the dawning of the fur trading era that the coast was thrown open to exploration as Russian, British and American ships came to ply the waters and the crews to trade trinkets with the natives for the prized fur of the sea otter.

The sea otter was soon driven near extinction and the traders moved inland. The white man brought with him his diseases which swept the native population in a series of devastating epidemics. The remaining Indians were pushed aside and placed on reservations.

The Northwest had been up for grabs among the Spanish, Russians and English but in the end it was taken by the Americans. The United States had few claims of discovery or exploration but gained control by flooding the land with American settlers who arrived to till the fertile soil.

The biographical section which follows presents the most notable personalities, the individuals who left their indelible mark on what was to become the great Oregon country....

Captain Benjamin L.E. Bonneville
(April 14, 1796—June 12, 1878)

Army officer and explorer Benjamin Bonneville was born in France and was brought to the United States by his parents when he was seven years old. He attended West Point, was graduated in 1815, served at various army posts until 1825 when he was detailed as escort to the French general Lafayette during his American visit. He later visited France as Lafayette's guest. Returning home in 1828 he was promoted to rank of captain and resumed active service until 1832 when he obtained a two-year leave of absence from the army. In the guise of an explorer seeking geographical information, but secretly surveying the possibilities of entering the fur trade, he made extensive travels through the Rocky Mountains and the Oregon country until returning to Independence on August 22, 1835, and learning he had been dropped from the army rolls. He went to Washington to begin a campaign for reinstatement. The following April President Jackson restored him to his captaincy. Bonneville continued his military career, serving with distinction in the Mexican War and the Civil War and was brevetted a brigadier general in 1865. He is buried at St. Louis, Missouri.

Captain William Clark
(August 1, 1770—September 1, 1838)

Soldier, explorer, co-leader of the Lewis and Clark expedition, William Clark was born in Virginia and received very little formal education. As a young man he joined his brothers and local militia fighting in the Indian wars. At the age of 21 he offered himself for regular service in the army and was commissioned lieutenant of infantry. Before resigning he served a period of four years, a portion of which was in the same division as Meriwether Lewis. He retired to private life and remained a civilian until 1803 when an unexpected letter arrived from his friend Captain Lewis, an invitation to accompany him in leading an expedition to the Pacific Ocean. The success of the expedition was due to the combined qualities of the two leaders. Clark had more enterprise, frontier experience and daring than Lewis. He was the mapmaker and artist, drawing birds, fish and animals with meticulous care and he kept a detailed journal of the daily happenings. After returning from the expedition Clark resigned from the army, married and settled in St. Louis. He was appointed Governor of Missouri Territory and later Superintendent of Indian Affairs, a position he held until his death.

Captain James Cook
(October 27, 1728—February 14, 1779)

British explorer and navigator James Cook was born at Marton, Yorkshire, England, joined the Royal Navy in 1755 and in four short years was master of his own ship. He was sent to the American east coast where he mapped the shores of Newfoundland and Labrador and charted the St. Lawrence River. In 1768 he sailed to the South Pacific where he made coastal surveys of New Zealand and Australia. His second voyage was to Antarctica in search of a continental land mass. The third expedition to the Pacific resulted in his discovery of the Sandwich (Hawaiian) Islands. On the morning of March 7, 1778, aboard the *Resolution*, he sighted the Oregon coast at Yaquina Bay, at a point he named Cape Foulweather. He cruised north along the coast. Upon returning to the Sandwich Islands for the winter he was killed by natives.

Sir Francis Drake
(c. 1543 — January 28, 1596)

British sea explorer and pirate Francis Drake was apprenticed at an early age on a coasting bark and learned his mastery of ship handling and pilotage in the Thames estuary and the English Channel. In 1567 he shipped as seaman with John Hawkins, a master in the slave trade, and in 1570 Drake commanded small private raiding expeditions to the West Indies. In 1577, in command of five ships, Drake departed on his most famous pirating voyage. Only the flagship *Pelican*, renamed the *Golden Hind*, successfully navigated the Strait of Magellan and steered up the Pacific coast of South America raiding harbors and ships and collecting a vast quantity of booty. Continuing to perhaps the 48th parallel north, Drake searched for a northwest passage and when it was not found he put in at a harbor somewhere on the coast, refitted the *Golden Hind* and sailed west across the Pacific, rounded the Cape of Good Hope and returned to England in 1580. In 1595 Drake and John Hawkins were employed in a large-scale raid on the Spanish West Indies. Both Drake and Hawkins died during the course of the voyage and were buried at sea.

General John Charles Fremont
(January 21, 1813 — July 13, 1890)

Western explorer, soldier and political leader John C. Fremont was born in Savannah, Georgia. He served in the navy but his real career began when he resigned from the navy to become a second lieutenant in the United States Topographical Corps to assist in a railroad survey. After surveying explorations to the headwaters of the Mississippi he obtained federal aid for a western journey. He first crossed the Rocky Mountains in 1842 and the following year, with an exploring party of about 40 men, he pushed his travels into the Oregon country. He reached the Columbia and on November 5, 1843, turned south down the east slope of the Cascades into Nevada and California. Again in 1845-46 he entered Oregon, coming up from the south, before returning to California and claiming it for the United States. He settled in California with his wife Jessie Benton, daughter of Senator Thomas Benton of Missouri, whom he had married in 1841. He represented California in the U.S. Senate; in 1856 he was an anti-slavery candidate for President but failed to win the election. He was a major-general in the Union army and was governor of Arizona Territory, 1878-81. He died in New York and is buried at Piedmont on the Hudson.

Captain Robert Gray
(May 10, 1755—1806)

Navigator, fur-trader and discoverer Robert Gray was born in Rhode Island. As a young man he took an active part in the naval service during the Revolutionary War. In 1787, in command of the sloop *Lady Washington* and with Captain John Kendrick and the *Columbia Rediviva*, Gray sailed from Boston on a fur trading voyage to the North Pacific. After a cargo of sea otter furs had been collected Gray took the *Columbia*, to whose command he had been transferred, to China and on to Boston to become the first American to carry the Stars and Stripes around the world. On Gray's second voyage to the North Pacific, on May 11, 1792, he sailed the *Columbia* through the line of foaming water and seething breakers guarding the entrance to the *River of the West*, naming it after his ship, *Columbia's River*. His discovery gave the United States its strongest claim to the Oregon country. Gray continued on to China and returned to Boston. He married in February 1794 and settled down to a quieter life as the master of a coastal shipping operation. In the summer of 1806, while on a voyage to Charleston, South Carolina, Gray died of yellow fever and was buried at sea.

Wilson Price Hunt
(March 20, 1783—April 13, 1842)

Explorer and fur trader Wilson Price Hunt was born in New Jersey but upon reaching legal age moved to St. Louis. He conducted a general store there until 1809 when he journeyed to New York and became a partner in Astor's Pacific Fur Company. He was put in charge of the overland expedition. On April 21, 1811, with Hunt as sole commander, the overland Astorians started up the Missouri River. At the Arikara villages the river route was abandoned and they struck west. On reaching the Snake River Hunt made the fateful decision to rid themselves of the horses and to navigate the river. The main body of Astorians broke into smaller groups that straggled into Astoria during the winter and spring of 1812. In August 1812 Hunt sailed in the *Beaver* to deliver a cargo of goods to the Russians in Alaska, receiving sealskins in payment which were taken to China. Learning of the declaration of war with Great Britain he returned to Astoria to find that his partners had already arranged to sell the post to the North West Company. April 3, 1814, he left the Columbia River for the last time. He returned to St. Louis and became a prosperous businessman.

Jason Lee
(June 28, 1803 — March 12, 1845)

Methodist missionary and Oregon pioneer Jason Lee was born in Vermont and experienced a religious conversion at age 23. He was ordained deacon and later elder in the Methodist Episcopal Church. The missionary society of this church chose him to head a mission to the West. Accompanied by his nephew and three lay assistants he left Independence, Missouri, with Nathaniel Wyeth's second expedition April 28, 1834. On September 15 the party arrived at Fort Vancouver where they were welcomed by Dr. John McLoughlin. The missionaries settled in the Willamette Valley, ten miles northwest of present-day Salem. In 1838 the Reverend Lee traveled to the East and returned to Oregon in 1840 with a party of fifty missionaries. It became apparent the hope of Christianizing the Indians was futile and efforts were directed toward the material upbuilding of the Oregon settlement. In 1844, having been superseded in his post, the Reverend Lee returned to the East. A conference of the Mission Board exonerated him of blame in the failure of the Willamette Valley mission but did not restore him to his post. That year his health failed. He contracted a severe cold and died. In 1906 his remains were brought to Oregon and, with appropriate ceremonies, reinterred at Salem.

Captain Meriwether Lewis
(August 18, 1774 — October 11, 1809)

Soldier, explorer, co-leader of the Lewis and Clark expedition, Meriwether Lewis was born in Virginia. In 1795 he enlisted in the regular army and served in the Indian wars. During one campaign he was a subordinate of William Clark. Lewis was serving at an outpost in Indian country in 1801 when his childhood friend and neighbor Thomas Jefferson was elected President of the United States. In the first week after his election Jefferson wrote Lewis offering him the post of his private secretary. Lewis accepted and spent two years at the White House where the matter of exploring a land route to the Pacific Ocean was frequently discussed. After the purchase of Louisiana an expedition was formed under the co-leadership of Lewis and William Clark. The success of the Lewis and Clark expedition (1804-1806) was due to the combined abilities of the two leaders. Lewis, however, was the true chief, the ultimate authority. He was intelligent and possessed a scientific mind and deep humane feelings for man and nature. Upon the return of the expedition President Jefferson appointed him governor of Louisiana. On October 11, 1809, on an overland trip to Washington, he met his death under mysterious circumstances at a tavern in the Tennessee mountains.

Sir Alexander Mackenzie
(c. 1764 — March 12, 1820)

Explorer, fur trader and the first white man to cross the American continent, Alexander Mackenzie was born in Scotland and emigrated to New York with his widowed father in 1774. Owing to the outbreak of the American Revolution he was sent to school in Montreal. He later joined a fur trading company that merged with the North West Company in 1787. He became a partner in the company and in 1789 he set out to explore the river flowing out of Great Slave Lake, the Mackenzie River, and followed it to the Arctic, proving the Northwest Passage did not exist. In 1793 he led an expedition westward over the Canadian Rockies to the Pacific Ocean, becoming the first European to cross the continent north of Mexico. His explorations were later the basis of the unsuccessful claim of Great Britain to the Oregon country. He returned to Scotland and was knighted by King George III.

Dr. John McLoughlin
(October 19, 1784 — September 3, 1857)

Canadian-born fur trader, chief factor of the Hudson's Bay Company and *Father of Oregon*, Dr. John McLoughlin was licensed to practice medicine in Quebec in 1803. That same year he joined the North West Company as a clerk and medical officer. He became a partner in the company in 1814. When the North West Company merged with the Hudson's Bay Company in 1821 he was placed in charge of the Rainy Lake District in Ontario and three years later was appointed Chief Factor of the Columbia District. He moved the headquarters from Fort George to Fort Vancouver. His duties were to monopolize the fur trade of the region, to impose permanent peace with the Indians and to prevent agricultural settlement of the region. He succeeded for a time but the gradual trapping out of the country and his friendliness to incoming missionaries opened the way to pioneer settlement. Eventually his empire crumbled. He retired in 1845. After the treaty was signed between the United States and England he became a U.S. citizen and resided at Oregon City until his death.

Joseph L. Meek
(1810—June 20, 1875)

Trapper and pioneer settler Joe Meek left his Virginia birthplace at age 18 and traveled to St. Louis where he fell in with W. L. Sublette's trapping expedition. For eleven years he trapped the Rocky Mountains in the company of frontiersmen Jim Bridger, Kit Carson, Tom Fitzpatrick, and William Sublette. By 1840 Meek was convinced the trapping era was over. He moved his family to Oregon and settled on the Tualatin Plains on the Willamette River. His dominating presence at Champoeg on May 2, 1843, helped win the Oregon country for the American side. He was made sheriff of the newly-formed Oregon territory and served in the 1846 and 1847 legislatures. After the Whitman massacre he was elected as the special messenger to carry the news to Washington and to ask for government protection from the Indians. He returned to Oregon to hang the five Indians convicted of the Whitman murders. When the Oregon bill passed in 1848 he was appointed marshal of the Oregon territory a position he lost in 1853 when Franklin Pierce was elected President of the United States. He spent the remainder of his days as a farmer.

Peter Skene Ogden
(1794—September 27, 1854)

Canadian-born explorer, fur trader Peter Skene Ogden was in the employ of the North West Company by his sixteenth birthday. He transferred to the Columbia District in 1818 and continued with the Hudson's Bay Company after the merger with the North West Company in 1821. He was placed in charge of the fur brigades which took him into almost every valley in eastern Oregon and southern Idaho to the head of Jefferson River in Montana. He was one of the first men to visit the Great Salt Lake and was first to traverse the valley of the Humboldt River, originally charted as Ogden's River, in northern Nevada. He named Mt. Shasta in northern California. About 1836 he was placed in charge of New Caledonia post on the Fraser River. In 1845 he replaced Dr. McLoughlin as chief factor at Fort Vancouver, a position he kept until his death. He is buried in Mountain View Cemetery, Oregon City.

Jedediah Strong Smith
(January 6, 1799 — May 27, 1831)

Explorer and fur trader Jedediah Smith left his New York birthplace at an early age and went in search of adventure. He signed on with General William Ashley Trading Co. in St. Louis in 1822 and became a mountain man. Four years later, along with two partners, he formed the Rocky Mountain Fur Company. On his first major expedition he came to Oregon from California and along the Umpqua River, July 14, 1828, his party was massacred by Indians. Only Smith and three others escaped and were able to make their way to Fort Vancouver. Dr. John McLoughlin sent a party to recover their horses, goods and furs. Smith sold the furs to the Company and returned east in March 1829. He was killed on the Cimarron by Comanche Indians.

Robert Stuart
(February 19, 1785 — October 29, 1848)

Fur trader and overland explorer Robert Stuart became a partner in John Jacob Astor's Pacific Fur Company. He sailed from New York on the *Tonquin* and arrived at the Columbia River in March 1811. He helped build Fort Astoria and was active in trading with the Indians. June 29, 1812, he and six companions departed Astoria with dispatches for Astor in New York. The party suffered greatly in crossing territory never before seen by white men. The route they followed, in time, became the route of the Oregon Trail. St. Louis was reached April 30 and New York on June 23, 1813. Stuart remained in the East, first as a traveling agent for Astor and later as an employee of Ramsay Crooks American Fur Company. He died in Chicago.

Captain George Vancouver
(June 22, 1757—May 1798)

Navigator and British explorer George Vancouver was born at King's Lynn, Norfolk, England, and enlisted in the British navy at age fifteen. He sailed with Captain James Cook on two voyages, one to the Antarctic, 1772-1774, and the other to the North Pacific, 1776-1780. In 1791 he was given command of an expedition to survey and map the northwest coast of America. Aboard his ship *Discovery* he sighted land on April 18, 1792. He cruised along the coast heading north. He missed spotting the signs of a great river and a few weeks later was informed of the Columbia River's existence by Captain Robert Gray. He verified Gray's claim but failed to cross the bar. He visited the region again in 1793 and 1794. He died at Petersham, Richmond, England.

Dr. Elijah White
(1806—April 3, 1879)

Early-day Oregon physician Dr. Elijah White was born in New York and educated at the medical college in Syracuse. In 1836 he was appointed by the Methodist Church as physician to its Willamette Valley mission but after his arrival differences with Jason Lee over mission policy caused him to resign. He returned to the States in 1841. The following year, after winning a political appointment as sub-Indian Agent for Oregon, he returned west leading the first large wagon train over the Oregon Trail. He attended the *Wolf Meeting* at Champoeg and spoke forcefully for rule by the American government. In 1845 he located a pass through the Coast range to the head of Yaquina Bay and later that year returned east bearing to the Congress a memorial of the Provisional Government. He returned to Oregon for a time in the 1850s but was commissioned a special Indian agent for the territory west of the Rockies and went to live in California.

Dr. Marcus Whitman
(September 4, 1802 — November 29, 1847)

Pioneer missionary and physician Marcus Whitman was born in New York, studied medicine there and spent eight years in practice before offering his services to the American Board of Commissioners for Foreign Missions. The Board sent him west in 1835 with the Reverend Samuel Parker to make a reconnaissance in Oregon. At Green River they met a delegation of Indians; the Reverend Parker contined west while Dr. Whitman returned to the East and prepared for the Oregon mission. In February 1836 he married Narcissa Prentiss and with the Reverend Henry Harmon Spalding and his wife Eliza and layman W. H. Gray they started west. One of the wagons was converted to a cart and brought as far as Fort Boise. The party founded two missions; Dr. Whitman choosing Waiilatpu in the Walla Walla Valley as the site of his mission. For a time it appeared the mission would be successful. But dissension among the missionaries forced Dr. Whitman to make a winter ride (1842-43) east to save his mission. The destruction of Waiilatpu occurred November 29, 1847, as Cayuse Indians swept through the mission killing Whitman, his wife, and twelve others.

Narcissa Prentiss Whitman
(March 14, 1808 — November 29, 1847)

Missionary to the Indians of the Northwest, Narcissa Prentiss Whitman was born in New York. A revival meeting in 1818 impelled her to join the Presbyterian Church and a further religious experience in 1824 moved her to pledge her life to missionary endeavor. She volunteered to the American Board of Commissioners for Foreign Missions to carry Christianity to the Indians in the far West but the Board was unwilling to commission *unmarried females*. However, Dr. Marcus Whitman, who had already been approved as a missionary, met her and proposed and they were married February 18, 1836. Also chosen to establish a mission in the West was the Reverend Henry Harmon Spalding and his wife Eliza Hart Spalding. Narcissa and Eliza became the first white women to cross the Rocky Mountains. After settling at Waiilatpu Narcissa gave birth to Alice Clarissa March 14, 1837. Two years later the little girl accidently drowned. Narcissa took in foster children, including all seven Sager children who were left orphans on the Oregon Trail in 1844. She made the mission a home until the fateful massacre November 29, 1847.

John Work
(1792—December 23, 1861)

Fur trader John Work was born in Ireland under the family name of Wark. Upon enlisting in the ranks of the Hudson's Bay Company, about 1814, his name appeared as Work on the Company rolls. He came from York Factory to the Columbia District in 1823 and was appointed chief trader in 1830. He led the annual fur brigades and ranked with Peter Skene Ogden in the worth of his services to the Company. From 1834 to 1835 he was in charge of the Company's vast shipping empire, with headquarters at Fort Vancouver. In 1835 he was sent to Fort Simpson and in 1849 to Victoria, B.C., where in 1850, with Peter Skene Ogden and James Douglas, he formed the Board of Managers of the Columbia Department. Work was a man of strong physique and great endurance but he finally succumbed to a reoccurrence of fever that had first stricken him while he was leading the Company fur brigades.

Nathaniel Jarvis Wyeth
(January 29, 1802—August 31, 1856)

Merchant and adventurer Nathaniel Wyeth left the family ice business in Massachusetts and embarked on a five-year attempt to exploit the Columbia river region for fish, furs, timber and agricultural resources. He departed Boston in 1832 with a company of 21 men and marched overland, reaching Fort Vancouver seven months later with eight men, the others having deserted or died enroute. This expedition failed because the supply ship was sunk at sea. Wyeth returned to the States and raised the necessary capital for a second expedition. Wyeth led Jason Lee and his missionaries west. He also established Fort Hall on the Snake River and Fort William on Wapato (Sauvie) Island. All of Wyeth's enterprises failed and he returned to Massachusetts in 1836 and re-entered the ice business.

Mt. Hood and the Columbia River

Historic Art Illustrations

Photographic Illustrations by Gildemeister

The Bear Wallow Story

The Bear Wallow Publishing Company was formed to help preserve our western heritage. The first book printed under the sign of the bear paw was **RENDEZVOUS** in 1978, an illustrated history of Northeast Oregon. The second book, **TRACES**, was published in 1980 and tells the story of the last few wagon pioneers. Today both books of limited printing are in great demand by collectors of rare and unique books.

The Bear Wallow Publishing Company stands for excellence in book publishing. Our pledge to the reader: To maintain the highest artistic quality, historical accuracy and deluxe publishing to insure each volume is a true work of art.

Carrying on this distinctive tradition is **WHERE ROLLS THE OREGON!**

Jerry & Cathy Gildemeister
Publishers, Photography, & Design

Jerry and his wife Cathy have a home-based studio in the sagebrush hills of Eastern Oregon. Jerry is the designer and co-author of **Where Rolls The Oregon** in addition to **Rendezvous, Union Centennial,** and **Traces**. He and Cathy work together, devoting their time to design, photography, and marketing in addition to publishing under **The Bear Wallow** name. Jerry and Cathy also provide consultation and production services to clients interested in self-publishing.

Rick Steber
Writer

Rick Steber, his wife Kristi and son Seneca Luke make their home in the Ochoco Mountains near Prineville, Oregon. For the past 13 years Rick has concentrated his writing on Oregon and the West and has authored, in addition to **Where Rolls The Oregon**, the books **Rendezvous, Union Centennial, Wild Horse Rider,** and **Traces**. Rick is a regular contributor to **Ruralite Magazine** and also writes the syndicated newspaper column **Oregon Country**.

Credits

Where Rolls The Oregon was designed by — Jerry Gildemeister.

Beaver artwork for cover embossing by — Don Gray.

Manuscript preparation and editing by — Kristi Steber.

Manuscript supplemental editing by — Linda Bird.

The text and maps were set in Goudy Oldstyle and Signet Roundhand by — Cathy Gildemeister.

Color prints from transparencies for color separations, copy/restoration of historic artwork and prints for halftones by — Cathy Gildemeister.

Color separations from prints and transparencies by — Pacific Color Plate Co. of Portland, Oregon.
> Scanning—Peter Hallinan.
> Proofing—David Staab.

The book was printed by — The Irwin-Hodson Company of Portland, Oregon.
> Production Manager — Doug Aasen.
>
> Line & Halftones, stripping, and plating by —
> George Brummer—Prep Department Foreman.
> Bob Koppler—Prep Department Assist. Foreman.
>
> 4-Color Press operation by —
> Steven Orlowski—Lead Pressman.
> Roger Jones—2nd Pressman.
> Charles Oaks—3rd Pressman.
>
> Bindery Foreman — Dave VanSwearingen.

Paper was supplied by — Fraser Paper Company of Portland, Oregon.
> Text paper is 80# Monaco Dull by — Midtec Paper Corporation of Kimberly, Wisconsin.
>
> The end sheets are 65# Natural Parchtone Cover by — French Paper Company of Niles, Michigan.

PMS ink for accent and Process for color, supplied by Cal/Ink of San Francisco, California.

The book was bound by — Lincoln & Allen Co. of Portland, Oregon.
> Books are bound with Imperial Bonded Leather by — Whitman Skivertex Ltd. of West Warwick, R. I.
>
> Embossing dies for the cover illustration by — Universal Stamping & Embossing Foils, Inc., of Kansas City, Kansas.

Production coordination by — Jerry & Cathy Gildemeister.

Library of Congress Cataloging-in-Publication Data

Steber, Rick 1946—
 Where Rolls The Oregon.

Writing: R. Steber; photography & design: J. Gildemeister.

Includes illustration index.

Summary: An accounting of the Oregon Country history from the first explorations through 1852...taken from journals, diaries and other writings...illustrated with color photography and historic art renderings.

 1. Oregon—History—to 1852. 2. Fur trade—Oregon—History—19th century. I. Gildemeister, Jerry, 1934— . II. Title.
 F880.S797 1985   979.5   85—9181
  ISBN 0-936376-03-1

Where Rolls The Oregon — ISBN 0-936376-03-1
— Other Publications by The Bear Wallow —

Rendezvous, First Printing © 1978 (*sold out*).   ISBN-0-936376-00-7.
Rendezvous, Second Printing © 1978. ISBN-0-936376-01-5.
Traces, Limited Printing © 1980 (*sold out*). ISBN-0-936376-02-3.

✎ In Parting ✎

I wish to thank Kristi Steber; Charles and Bettye Steber; Frank L. Gast, Rick Chrisinger and staff of the Crook County Library; Yvonne Katter and the reference staff of the Deschutes County Library; Oregon State Library and Interlibrary Loan Service; and Gary Clark.

Rick Steber

With thanks and appreciation to the staff of Pierce Library at Eastern Oregon State College for their assistance in research for this project.....to Steve Orlowski, lead pressman whose help was invaluable on the past two book projects—yet whose name was not mentioned in the credits.....and finally, a very special thank you to my wife, partner and co-worker—Cathy, whose help, understanding and endurance made this project possible.

Jerry Gildemeister